Nicola,

GO Pro!

Ryan Blair

I'm giving you this book because:

NOTHING to LOSE

NOTHING to LOSE

How to Find Your Passion, Fire Your Boss, and Become an Entrepreneur

Ryan Blair

with *New York Times* best-selling author Don Yaeger

Published by Nothing to Lose Publishing.

Nothing to Lose Publishing
6300 Wilshire Blvd., Suite 1440
Los Angeles, CA 90048
www.NothingtoLose.com

To order additional copies, call 800-759-6839.

Cover and interior design: JENNINGS DESIGN/www.jenningsdesignonline.com

Cover photo: Glam Rock Photography

ISBN-13: 978-0-615-33874-3

LCCN: 2009942028

Printed in the United States of America.

10 9 8 7 6 5 4 3 2 1

To my son, Ryan Reagan Blair

CONTENTS

ACKNOWLEDGMENTS

I have many people in my life whom I want to thank. Everything I have learned, I have learned from someone. I first want to thank God for giving me the faith necessary to overcome many obstacles, most of which were self-imposed. And second, I thank my entire family, since they are the people who kept me from the edge of many cliffs. The first person I need to thank in my family is Kasie Head. If it were not for you, Kasie, I never would have written this book. Your encouragement and belief in me has given me more than I could ever put in words. On April 6, 2009, you gave me the greatest gift I have ever known, my son Ryan Reagan Blair. You continue to inspire me every day by being an amazing partner and mother. I would also like to thank my mother, Erla Hunt. Mom, you kept me positive in the face of great adversity, and you led me out of it. I also want to thank Robert Hunt for being my first role model and for teaching me how to think like an entrepreneur. Bob, the beliefs you taught me have been my foundation for success. Thank you, Stephanie Gager, for being the best big sister a little brother could ever have. Steph, thank you for taking me in when I had nowhere else to go. Last, I want to thank my grandmother, Wini, for instilling in me spirituality and teaching me unconditional love.

I also want to thank the people most responsible for making this book a reality. Don Yaeger, thank you for having the confidence in me to pass up many projects to put my stories and philosophies on paper. Coach Dale Brown, I appreciate you for your mentorship and for introducing me to Don and Coach John Wooden, two people who have added indescribable value to my my life. I also want to thank Tiffany Brooks, Erica Jennings, Shannon Logan, and Grace Manzano for your hard work on this project. A special thank you to Jade Charles and Joe Perez for their incredible social media skills.

Many thanks to every team member of every company I've been a part of. It is because of your talent and commitment that we have been successful. And to my partners in ViSalus, Nick Sarnicola and Blake Mallen, thank you for bringing me on as a partner and for putting up with me along the way. You guys are the most talented and dedicated people I've ever worked with. I also want to thank the entire ViSalus community for believing in a vision greater than all of us and for your hard work to see that vision into reality.

Last, I want to thank every person who ever invested in my ventures; it is because of your willingness to take a risk that the entrepreneurial world goes round.

PROLOGUE

Why I Wrote This Book, and Why You Should Read It

When I sat down to write this book in December 2008, the president's economic advisor announced that the American economy had fallen into a "depression." The announcement was paired with a report from the United States Department of Labor that more than 533,000 Americans lost their jobs in November 2008, and 1.9 million Americans became unemployed during that calendar year. We entered the "Great Recession."

In the private sector, major retailers started to fold, and construction dried up. States struggled to balance budgets, affected by a housing-bust-created decreased tax base, which led to salary cuts and the elimination of many positions across the country.

By June 2009, the national unemployment rate was the highest in more than twenty-five years: 9 percent and rising. By the end of the month, the Department of Labor released unemployment numbers for all the municipalities it tracked—and the statistics were frightening. Cleveland, Louisville, Orlando, and Tampa reported unemployment at 10 percent. The Las Vegas, Sacramento, and San Jose metropolitan areas reported over 11 percent. The Detroit area reported almost 15 percent unemployment, and Yuma, Arizona, logged in at over 23 percent. By September 2009, 9.8 million jobs had been lost in the US economy, and *The New York Post* reported that the jobless rate for people between the ages of sixteen and twenty-four was 52.2 percent, the highest level since before World War II.

Of the unemployed, nearly 5.5 million exhausted their unemployment benefits in the last year, and another 1.3 million stood to lose their benefits by the end of 2009. Clearly, the problem was neither isolated to one geographical region, nor was it contained to one or two troubled industries. This situation knew no boundaries and was no respecter of social status. Blue-collar and white-collar jobs were both being slashed, and competition for the limited number of open positions that did exist was incredibly fierce.

 **Keep in mind that sixteen of today's Dow 30 companies were founded during a recession or a depression. Corporate icons, such as General Electric, Johnson & Johnson, Proctor & Gamble, and Disney, were formed under economic circumstances much as we see today.**

Chances are, these numbers I just quoted are more than just figures on a page for you—it's real life. Maybe you're anticipating a pink slip any day now, or maybe you already received one. Maybe you are ready to move on to a new job but are afraid to hit the market, given the economic outlook. Or maybe you have looked at the current climate and realized that, with prices dropping and inventories high, this might be the perfect time to jump at a new opportunity to create, invest, restructure, and venture out on your own.

The fact is that there is a silver lining in those bleak unemployment numbers. History tells us that tens of thousands of Americans will use this moment of adversity as fuel to do something they might otherwise not have done: chase a passion and start a business. For some of you reading this now, the decision might have been made for you when your company downsized.

For some, now may be the most feasible time in a decade to begin a business on a limited budget. Either way, you have NOTHING TO LOSE.

Twenty-five years from now, the history books will show that in this moment, some of the greatest companies of our generation were born from that nothing-to-lose mindset. Keep in mind that sixteen of today's Dow 30 companies were founded during a recession or a depression. Corporate icons, such as General Electric, Johnson & Johnson, Proctor & Gamble, and Disney, were formed under economic circumstances much as we see today.

There are three reasons why I know this is the time for you to make your move. First, an economy like this presents many companies and consumers with problems they have never faced before. Finding solutions to those problems is an entrepreneur's dream. Second, everything you need to start a business—from office space to employees—is available at the best prices in years. Finally, an economy in crisis turns the status quo on its ear. When things are good, it is often tough for an ingenious entrepreneur to gain the attention of market leaders. In tough times, that trend is reversed. If you are ready to start over, ready to make your nothing-to-lose attitude work for you, then this book is for you.

This is not a book full of reassuring promises or tantalizing "confidential" information for getting rich quick. Here is the one secret I can offer you: there isn't one secret. Anyone who tells you he or she has it is selling fool's gold. This book is designed to serve as a guide for people who are willing to do whatever it takes—hard work, long hours, sweat equity, dedication, and reality checks—to take their vision from paper to pavement.

I know that some people roll their eyes when they scan my bio because they focused only on the result: I started and built six multimillion-dollar companies by the time I was thirty. *He's a con man—just one of those get-rich-quick guys! He must have been born into it, and he inherited the connections and capital. It probably all came easy to him.* Believe me, I have heard it all. The plain and simple truth is that I learned to act when others wouldn't, and I learned how to work hard.

As a former juvenile delinquent, nothing came easy. The youngest of six, I grew up in a comfortable middle-class home until my father became wrapped up in the drug scene. By the time he left, my mother was struggling to recover from depression and the abuse he'd piled on her, and one by one, my older siblings had started to go down the same path. In and out of prison, back on the streets—it sometimes felt like our family had a deadbeat identity that we couldn't shake.

 **The gap between the classes is growing. The rich are getting richer, and the poor are getting poorer. Bankers are sucking the economy dry, working only with the safe subjects where there is no risk. Is that what we gave them our taxpayer money for?**

I was different, though, because I gravitated more toward gangs than I ever did toward drugs—not that gangs were a better option. I did not join by choice; gangs were a requirement of the neighborhood where I lived. I spent quite a bit of my formative years in and out of juvenile detention, convinced that I was a victim and that criminal behavior was my only option. But through a series of life-changing events and perspective-changing lessons, I was finally able to get off the path to nowhere.

And that is the core message of this book: take this adversity and do great things. In the following chapters, I will outline what I have learned from mentors, experience, and a lot of trial and error. I don't simply want to encourage your inner entrepreneur; I want to give you a road map, complete with actions to take and pitfalls to avoid. What you will find is a series of suggestions for hard skills with practical application.

I can't guarantee profitability. No reputable person can. But I can offer real-life stories of success and failure, and I can share what I learned from each venture and from each mentor that I was privileged enough to have take an interest in me. And their message is always quite simple: there is no shortcut to success.

By the time I had finished writing this book in December 2009, I went back and reread my prologue. The unemployment numbers hadn't changed much. Because marked job growth usually follows rather than precedes an economic turnaround, the aftereffects were likely to linger for quite a while longer. I knew that I had to rally the American people. I sat down and wrote a piece that summed up the sentiment behind the purpose of this book. I called it the Manifesto of the Entrepreneur:

The gap between the classes is growing. The rich are getting richer, and the poor are getting poorer. Bankers are sucking the economy dry, working only with the safe subjects where there is no risk. Is that what we gave them our taxpayer money for?

Our jobs have gone away and our American dream has been foreclosed on, as our overdraft fees mount, and the wait on the phone with the unemployment office gets longer and longer. The Good Old Boys network—bankers and politicians—make sure their money goes round, but what about the average workers? What about the 15 million unemployed?

Don't you feel the friction? Aren't you angry at the imperialists that sold us our overpriced homes, the lit-fused debt instruments, and easy money offers that were swiftly delivered to our colleges and our mailboxes? The faulty structures and sleazy salesmen? Yes, we accepted their terms. And they knew we would.

Our generation had it all, and now it has nothing. Nothing to lose.

I have a plan to restore the American dream, to make the liars pay. Innovate them out of existence. It doesn't matter what your education is or isn't. Democrat or Republican. What matters is your mindset. The dedication to finding a way to make profits while keeping promises, to create jobs, to create companies, and to be part of companies that are finding ways to cut out the people who collapsed our economy in the first place—connecting us to the tools we need to build a new America.

One where authenticity commands respect of the powers that lead and your contribution to society isn't taxed, but rather invested in. Where the more jobs you create, and the more problems you solve, the more you're rewarded. Where you're not penalized for making it. Or writing blind checks to programs and systems designed by our parents' parents—for compromised solutions, instead of finding the root of the problem and solving it.

We have no real influence over the politicians, and they aren't going to solve this problem for us. So who is going to create jobs for the 50 percent of college graduates out there looking for work? Who is going to create jobs for the 15 million unemployed? Not the existing Corporate America, because as soon as the big corporations and government-subsidized, stimulus-backed businesses have squeezed every ounce of energy out of their American workers, they are not going to hire back the dead weight they cut. Instead, they will outsource the new jobs to countries that will work for pennies on the dollar and reap billions in profits at the expense of the working taxpayers who kept their business alive and their hundred-million-dollar compensation packages.

Our generation needs to solve this problem! And I'm not just talking to the baby boomers, Gen X, or Gen Y. I'm addressing Gen E—the entrepreneurial generation. The creative generation. The stuff America was built on. Bootstraps and ingenuity. Mavericks and risk-takers. We need to start turning our ideas into jobs, our purpose into products, and our services into service. It's time to stop fighting for jobs and start creating them. We have to get off the sidelines and start leading this revolution.

So if you're an entrepreneur, or you know that it's your calling, I invite you to read this book. I ask you to give this book to anyone you know who should be an entrepreneur, too. Because if you're anything like the rest of us, then you have nothing to lose.

apps.facebook.com/nothingtolose

We've made it easy for you to create your own board of advisors on Facebook. Check it out at apps.facebook.com/nothingtolose!

- Promote your business
- Set up your board of advisors
- Network with other Nothing to Lose CEOs

CHAPTER 1

MY LIFE

I didn't start out at the bottom—but I reached it quickly.

Long before I became a millionaire entrepreneur, I was a punk with a juvenile criminal record, street gang experience, and a lot of emotional scarring from years of abuse from my father. My teenage years were hardly the typical starting point for a normal, productive life, let alone a successful business career. Turns out, that didn't matter.

The first decade or so of my life was actually unremarkable in a pleasant, upper-middle-class kind of way. My family lived in a small, comfortable community in Southern California. No one was exceptionally wealthy where we lived; but just a town or two away were the billionaires' hot spots, and a town or two in the other direction was the ghetto. So we basically knew where we were situated on the ladder, and we were all pretty content with that.

My family had a pool, lots of nice clothes, and at Christmas, a new bike or scooter if I wanted one—we were doing pretty well, by most people's standards. And then, just as I was hitting my middle school years, my dad got hooked on drugs.

He'd always had a pretty intense personality. My five older siblings had already learned to watch out for his temper; as the baby of the family, I had learned that lesson almost as soon as I learned to walk. But he wasn't a bad guy.

That's the thing that always gets me. When people hear my story now, they often say to me, "Your dad sounds like a terrible person." He was terrible to live with, once his life really started falling apart. But he wasn't a terrible person—not at first, anyway. In fact, I learned a lot from him.

 **My dad paid me a dollar per bag of weeds I pulled from the yard. If I could convince the neighborhood kids to do it for 50 cents, then I could turn a profit by having several kids fill a number of bags at once, while I worked on another paying chore.**

For example, when I was a kid, I was rewarded through compensation. If I got a base hit playing baseball, there would be a certain prize at the end of it, like a new batting glove. I was always competing for something. It was my dad who offered these rewards—he was the first person to instill in me a work ethic and a risk–reward mentality.

He didn't believe in allowances; he believed in chores, and he paid me to do them. If I washed the cars, I got five dollars per car. If I mowed the lawn, I got paid for that, too. Maybe it's not the best arrangement for every family, but it certainly worked for me. I came to associate effort with profit.

But it was more than just profit. Dad taught me about the pride that comes with hard work, too. He would always give me recognition among his friends and coworkers as he told them what a strong worker I was and how much I earned; as a result, I would try to work more and more. He bragged to one of his friends about my paper routes, so I decided to grow that aspect of my work routine, and soon I had three paper routes.

I also learned how to maximize my earning opportunities. My dad paid me a dollar per bag of weeds I pulled from the yard. If I could convince the neighborhood kids to do it for 50 cents, then I could turn a profit by having several kids fill a number of bags at once, while I worked on another paying chore. Thanks to my father, it really was instilled in me early on to have ambition, motivation, and hunger for money.

But the psychological aspects of his poor upbringing, his insecurities, and his issues ended up getting the better of him. That's what ultimately pushes everyone who goes in that direction, isn't it? His "issues" pushed him into drugs, and everything else spiraled out of control.

My dad was middle-class, but he lived as if he were among the elite. He leveraged himself as so many Americans do—financed his cars, borrowed to buy his house, spent his last dollars on making our house look pretty—to make himself feel more important. He lived beyond his means and started using drugs to cope with it all; that was his undoing.

He ultimately failed because he never really had a deeper sense of purpose. He was proud of his kids for working so hard; he had a gorgeous trophy wife; and he had a beautiful house, beautiful cars, and all the things that a person could want. But he didn't have a deep sense of purpose in his life. As a result, he threw it all away, and he chased himself out of our lives.

The problem was simple: he got addicted to drugs. He stuck around just long enough to drag everyone else down along with him, and then he was gone. At the time, there were three children still at home—my older siblings had already left home. As if my dad's failure gave them the excuse they were looking for, their lives seemed to fall apart as well. One sister moved in with a druggie boyfriend; another ran away and lived on the streets for a while. Finally, it was just my parents and me. That's when the bottom really fell out of my life.

My dad used to have a gun collection, and, being a naive kid, I showed the guns off to my friends. A few days later, the older brother of one of my friends broke into the house and stole them all. I didn't find out until several years later who had actually been involved; at the time, it didn't matter. Dad thought I did it.

By this time, the drugs were making him paranoid and even more violent. He swore I'd stolen them and sold them, and he threatened to kill me if I didn't give them back. After all I'd seen, I knew that I didn't want to stick around for the repercussions. It was dangerous. That night I called my sister and told her, "He's promising to kill me."

As grateful as I was for my sister's offer to stay with her, the new situation presented its own set of challenges. She was living with a musician at the time.

He might have been an aspiring rock star—there are a lot of those in Southern California—but he certainly didn't have rock star money. They were residing in a tiny, dirty house and surviving on macaroni and cheese, which was all either one could seem to afford.

When I arrived at their house, they walked a sleeping bag out to a dilapidated little shed in the back, tossed it in, and said, "Here you go." It was a shack. It had doors, it had a window, and it had holes in the walls. There's no nicer way to describe it. But I was away from my dad and, at the moment, that was the most important thing.

A few days later, I went to the thrift store for rolls of carpet that people would donate after they redecorated their houses. There were a couple of pieces that were large enough to serve as insulation, so I pinned them over the walls to try to block out some of the weather. It was Southern California, so it wasn't the most extreme climate; but even so, it got cold at night, so I ran pieces of carpet over the doors to try to keep out the wind. I did have a tiny space heater, though, and the electricity to run it on, and that was what helped me make it through the winter.

But the weather was not my biggest enemy. That distinction belonged to the lice that infested the shack.

It didn't matter how much I showered or what I tried to do to my hair to get rid of them; the next day they would be back. I could feel them crawling down my head and onto my back while I slept on the floor on the beat-up mattress that eventually replaced my sleeping bag. Finally, in an act of desperation to be rid of the lice, I decided to shave my head. Michael Jordan's dome gave shaved heads a big boost in the '90s, but the look hadn't really come on the scene yet. Shaved heads were definitely not cool at that time. The favorite taunt at school became, "Ryan Blair has no hair!" in an annoying, sing-songy cadence that poked every nerve in my body, even as I tried to ignore it.

For close to a year, I lived in that miserable little shack. I felt that I couldn't go home as long as my father was there and still an addict, and my mother clearly wasn't planning to leave my father anytime soon. So I stayed put, feeling that even though I'd been the one to leave, I'd been abandoned by both of them.

The shack that was Ryan's home for nearly a year.

Finally, when the principal of my school, Dr. Judy Dunlap, called me into her office to talk to me about my failing grades, I spilled it all: the issues with my parents, my current living situation—I told her everything. Suddenly, my grades were the last thing on her mind. "We have to call social services. We have no choice," she explained. "What you are telling me is that you are in danger."

By law, the principal also had to get me to a psychologist, and she demanded that my mother come along, too. After I recounted to the shrink everything that had gone wrong with my family over the past few years, he looked my mom in the eye and said, "*You* are the abuser."

My mother was shocked. "It's his father!" she insisted. "He's the bastard! He's the beater and he beats me, too."

The psychologist just shook his head and told her, "You're a grown adult, and you are letting your child go through this. You are negligent by law, and we are going to take him away if you don't make things right immediately. You have no choice but to act right now."

This made my mother reevaluate the situation for the first time because, in her mind, she was the victim, not me. And she *was* a victim. She bore many punches that I never got because she stepped in front of my father. I remember her face being black and blue, and that she'd told people she'd been in a car accident. I remember watching him throw the punches, and I remember him dragging me into the room to have me watch—as a lesson for me to never stand up to him. I remember once seeing him point a gun to her head and tell her he was going to kill her if she didn't quit crying. There is no question that my mother was a victim. But in her mind, she had endured all of the abuse so that I wouldn't have to; it never occurred to her that I was being damaged anyway.

She finally agreed with the psychologist that she had to take action, so she called my father that night and told him, "They are going to put Ryan in foster care, so you need to leave. I'm bringing Ryan back to the house because he's living in unfit conditions, and they are going to inspect here."

That was what broke her from him—that the state was going to intervene. She took a stand, and we hoped it meant turning a corner for everyone. But after about three months, my father started dropping by again and was as violent as ever, coming after both my mother and me. Whenever the attacks would start, I'd run out of the house and back to my sister's, which still seemed like a better option.

My mother was determined to protect me this time, though. She found a little one-bedroom place next door to my sister and somehow managed to scrape together the $500 deposit without my dad's knowledge. One day she told me to pack my belongings, so I piled into the car all of the things that matter most to a thirteen-year-old: my Nintendo, my CDs, and my clothes—all the trappings of my family's pleasant, middle-class life that, in the end, was just a sham.

We moved everything over to the new house and then went back to the old house for one last carload of my mother's belongings. By the time we returned, our new place had been gutted. Everything inside was gone. Someone had watched us carrying in boxes, waited for us to leave, and then broke in and took it all.

My mom was hysterical. Here she was going out on a limb in a last, desperate effort to break away from our abusive situation, and we were robbed blind on the first day. The police weren't able to help us very much, either. The officer who arrived in response to our call advised us not to file a report. We lived right

The one-bedroom home Ryan shared with his mother.

next to a park where all the vagrants and gangsters hung out. We saw scary-looking men congregating there, some with teardrop tattoos by their eyes and prison tattoos all over their arms.

They watched us going in and leaving—just eyed us in a way that made my skin crawl. "If I take a report from you," the officer told us, "they are going to know you told on them, and they're going to get revenge. I'd suggest for everyone's safety that you just let it go."

My mother was crying from the sheer helplessness she felt at that point. The officer reached into his pocket, handed my mother a twenty-dollar bill, and said, "I'm really sorry this happened to you." Then he turned to me and said, "Hey, son, you do not want to tangle with those guys. Do not get mixed up with them, whatever you do."

And that was the welcome we received to our new life.

Dad eventually found out where we were, but I guess he figured he was better off without us; he never made an effort at that point to get clean. Because my mother had taken me away to try to protect me, walking away seemed like a good idea to him, too. He disappeared from my life for the next fourteen or fifteen years.

Mom and I both tried to make the best of the situation. She got a job at the deli of a local supermarket and tried to break free from her own problem drinking; I would play basketball at the park to try to keep out of trouble. I didn't do a very good job, though—trouble was all around me, and I figured it was easier to join in than to fight it. Whenever I'd be out shooting baskets, guys would approach me and ask my gang affiliation. I told them I didn't have one—the whole idea of street gangs was still pretty new to me.

But I quickly saw how the system worked, how the street lords kept themselves in power through influence and manipulation. I observed how the older people used bribery and fear to get the younger kids to do their crimes, and I saw how the young people willingly went along with it because it seemed like the only power structure that had any kind of respect in the neighborhood.

It was a flashy, angry, tempting world of getting what you want and not caring about the risks. The risks were part of the esteem—the more brazen your crime, the more respect you got. As a scrawny kid who felt powerless against everything going on in my life, that appealed to me. I don't blame anyone or anything else but myself for my choices. But I do understand how a competitive, tenacious, and confused person could easily allow himself to get caught up in it all.

My behavior and grades plummeted again. This time, I was an eighth grader, and I got kicked out of school. Two months into ninth grade, I was asked to leave high school, too. I wasn't big—my growth spurt was still a year or two away—but I was mouthy and always arguing with the teachers to the point that they felt threatened.

Every day I came to class with a chip on my shoulder, thinking, "None of you could ever understand what I'm going through, so how dare you tell me what to do? It's interesting that you tell me one day, algebra is going to be important to me. Do you understand that in my life right now, my survival is what's important to me? And you're telling me it's really important that I listen to history? I'm going to go home and get jumped on my way back or have a gun pointed in my face, and I'm supposed to care about what you have to say?"

The teachers immediately diagnosed me as a problem kid. They fought to get me Ritalin for ADD and Prozac for depression; they fought to get me out of the classroom. That was fine with me. It was easier to hang out on the streets, anyway. Breaking into cars to steal stereo equipment and resell it was easier than working for what I wanted, so I figured that was a better route for me.

I landed in juvenile detention a couple of times, which actually ended up being a positive thing in the long run, because it was there that I discovered my fascination with computers, which in turn led to the development of my first company. But that would be years down the road.

The other positive thing in my life during that period was Randy Pentis. He was a local cop with the type of face that only a cop could have—all hard lines and ill humor. When I was a teenager, the sight of this face meant only one thing: the certainty of unavoidable punishment. One glimpse of this man would send my gang scattering down the street like billiard balls in a break, ducking behind buildings and flying around corners. I was desperate to get away from the police officer who made it his personal agenda to keep me from making the mistakes I was determined to make.

I remember Officer Pentis best for the grip of his hand on the back of my shirt, and for the time he dragged me up the walkway in the middle of the night to wake my mother and explain to her why her son wore the bandana, the sneakers, the belt, and the rest of the gang attire. Randy Pentis is the man who arrested me—more than once. And he challenged me to do better for myself than I was at that time. But the results of that lesson were years down the road, too. At that moment, I was an out-of-control teenager who seemed destined for prison.

Then my mom started dating a man named Robert Hunt; with his influence, our lives turned around.

Over a few years, my mother had moved up from making minimum wage as a deli clerk to being the department manager, and she met Robert when he came to the store as a customer. He was a successful, stable businessman who owned his own real estate company. He was smart, kind, and sober, and he took a special interest in me at a time when I desperately needed a strong male figure in my life.

They hadn't been dating very long when Robert invited my mother and me to move into his house. He made the offer after coming over to our place to pick up Mom for a date and being absolutely horrified at where we lived. My mother was a little hesitant, but Robert explained that it would get me away from the crowd I'd been running with, out of the dangerous neighborhood where we were living, and it would give him a chance to have a more direct influence over my life. He knew that at the rate I was going, getting out was the only shot we had at success. My mother and I realized that we had nothing to lose.

 **Looking around me, I started to observe how people who were legitimately wealthy lived—I realized that it all came down to the work that they put into themselves and their professions.**

I was seventeen years old when the move happened, and Robert insisted that I live with him and my mother until I was at least eighteen. I agreed to the arrangement because I didn't really have an alternative.

I'll never forget the day I pulled up to the gates of Robert's beautiful, upscale neighborhood in my '78 Toyota Corolla station wagon. One of the security guards recognized me; his name was Terry, and he ran one of the few legitimate businesses in my old neighborhood. We'd bring him our recyclables to weigh, then he'd give us a voucher for the supermarket.

"What the hell are you doing here?" Terry grumbled at me as I slowed my car. I told him I lived there now. "Get the hell out of here! You don't live here," he said.

I grinned, assured him that I really did live there, and then added, "You work for me now." He laughed. As he waved me through the gate, I realized just how much my entire life had changed.

Looking around me, I started to observe how people lived—not when they were burglarizing cars for a living, and not when they were only pretending to have a lot of disposable income, but how people who were legitimately wealthy lived. I realized that it all came down to the work that they put into themselves and their professions. I realized they had a system, too. A system of wealth, unlike the system that ran the streets.

One time I was driving my stepdad's car to get it washed, and several older gentlemen approached me and asked casually, "So what do you do?" I guess they thought I was a celebrity or an athlete to have a car like that as a teenager. And with that experience, and others that followed, I got to observe how society attaches labels to you. I started wearing polo shirts and dressing nicely. Girls at school were suddenly allowed to date me, whereas before I'd been off-limits to most of the "nice girls." I looked like the son of Robert Hunt. No one seemed to know, or care, that he didn't raise me from birth to right where I was. For all they were concerned, I was the protégé of Robert Hunt, a very successful real estate entrepreneur—and I worked for him.

To me, that really was what mattered—the idea that I *worked* for him; that even as a teenager, I was a professional. Reaching way back to my childhood, before the gangs and the violence and the drugs, I found that work ethic my father had instilled in me, and I dusted it off.

My first job with Robert was running errands and doing general chores around the office that needed doing. After a while, he gave me other tasks, the main one being that I had to do process serving for eviction notices to families who weren't paying their rent, three-day notices ordering tenants to pay rent or quit the property, and foreclosure notices.

Some people think of that line of business as being too harsh, or that all I had experienced over the past few years might make it difficult for me to do that, but I saw things differently.

People were falling behind on their payments either because they'd gotten into properties greater than what they could afford or because they made bad spending decisions and chose to fund the illusion of prosperity rather than meeting their real-life obligations. And it wasn't just some faceless corporation that got stuck paying for their mistakes, it was Robert—my mentor. When someone didn't pay the rent for three months, that deficit didn't just disappear. It came out of Robert's pocket. So, in essence, each delinquent tenant was passively robbing him.

Ryan heading to his first day of work at the call center.

I took my job seriously. I wanted every family to have a fair chance to get caught up on their payments or to find a new place to live, so I made sure I delivered every notice promptly and respectfully. Many people got their affairs in order and nothing further came of it. Others simply refused to leave, and at that point, my job was to make them move.

During this time, I was eighteen years old, 6'3", 240 pounds, and I'd spent a lot of time in rough company. I never used physical force with my job. Robert wouldn't have tolerated that. I did cut an imposing figure, though, and I wanted to prove myself not only to my stepdad, but to myself, as well. Each time I'd pull up to a house, I'd brace myself for a confrontation. People talk about the significance of sweat equity when they were first starting out. I know a thing or two about it—I had literal sweat equity trickling down my back and dripping down my forehead, making my eyes sting.

It wasn't long before my hard work paid off, and I was offered a job at another company. It was called Logix, and I started out as a customer service representative answering about 120 inbound telephone calls a day. Starting salaries were around $6.00 per hour, and we'd get a small bonus every time we saved an account or got someone to upgrade. In that call center, I learned a lot. I saw the turnover, the hirings and firings, and the training process. I saw a system.

Logix had a data center that was designed to support its call center downstairs. I always wanted to go to work there because I loved computers, so one day I just asked if I could cover a swing shift for the data center. That experience allowed me to bond with the manager of that group, and he offered to transfer me from the call center into the data center.

I made the switch, got a raise to $6.50 per hour, and learned how to change the backup tapes and reboot computers if they went down; just basic stuff. But I didn't see it as menial; I saw it as a tremendous learning opportunity to figure out how the company worked on a number of different levels. I was a student, a sponge, reading every book on computer science that I could find and simply immersing myself in the subject.

In the meantime, I also started going to the community college because Robert Hunt had a rule that if I lived underneath his roof, I had to complete high school, go to college, and get a job. I didn't want to work for him any-more because I wanted to venture out on my own into the field of computers, so I took it upon myself to learn every last thing I could from classes, books, and articles, and from talking to experts.

Because of my street-smart leadership skills and my salesmanship skills, I was soon the lead data-center technician. Next, I was made the supervisor of the center, and then I was made the manager of the center. Finally, at the age of twenty and after only about three years with Logix, I was made a vice president. I went from making $6.00 an hour to making over $100,000 a year. I will always be indebted to Keith Howington, the CEO of Logix, for giving me the opportunity and mentorship at Logix. He taught me many lessons that I still apply to this day.

At that point, I realized that there wasn't any kind of insider knowledge to succeed at business. It just took two indispensable qualities: hard work and dedication. And not long afterward, I launched my first company.

So what was the point of dedicating an entire chapter to explaining my life before I became an entrepreneur? There are several reasons.

First, I want to be honest. I don't have a sterling past. Chances are, you're coming from your own set of damages and bad experiences. Use those to propel yourself to better things. Learn from them. If I can make it—starting out as a thug kid to ending up as a stable citizen who enjoys financial success—anyone can do it.

Second, I had people who were willing to mentor me, to give me another chance, and to let me prove myself. Don't be too proud to accept help. That's going to be one of the most important aspects of growing your business, and you need to be okay with that early on.

Finally, I want to emphasize that we are not defined by our circumstances. Whatever situation you might find yourself in, it's easy to allow that to become the lens through which you define yourself. You are stronger than whatever circumstances you're facing. Remember that potential is the one power you always have, and start from there to move forward.

CHAPTER 2

FIND YOUR DRIVER

The Death Cycle. Day in and day out, you get up before dawn to make a grueling commute to a green-light-tinged building, where you spend eight, nine, or ten hours a day working at a job that doesn't fulfill you, doesn't exhibit your personal talents, and makes you dread each moment you have to spend thinking about it. By the time you get home to your family, you are too drained to enjoy their company and too tired from thinking of the day of drudgery ahead to make the most of your free time. The Death Cycle.

How do you break out of it?

The first step to consider, once you've determined that you have nothing to lose by taking a shot at entrepreneurial thinking, is to figure out what motivates you.

You know the drill. In any crime show, the detective characters always ask these questions, *What was the motive? What drove the person to act?* Obviously, we're talking about something far better than a criminal mindset here, but I think it's essential to recognize how motivation truly surrounds us in every aspect of our lives—from personal choices to human interactions with one another, and within society at large.

Motivation can steer both our short-term and long-term decision making. It can affect our personality, temperament, and interests. It is one of the most powerful forces in our lives—and it is often subconscious. We rarely stop to question exactly what our motivation is in each circumstance, but I believe that by simply taking stock of the motives behind our professional decisions, each subsequent move will be more deliberate, directed, and effective.

 **Why do *you* want to step out on your own? Something must be driving this decision, and it's something inside you. Without a clear answer to this question, it will be nearly impossible to build a viable business. But once you determine your driver, it becomes the jumping-off point for everything that follows as you become an entrepreneur.**

In fact, the very first step in creating your business is rooted in motivation. You need to determine honestly what your motivation is—what drives you to want to become an entrepreneur? "I lost my job and I need something to do" isn't going to cut it as an answer here, because that mindset allows something external to be in control and allows your circumstances to define you. That can be hugely detrimental to your business plan. There has to be something deeper than that. Why do *you* want to step out on your own? Something must be driving this decision, and it's something inside you. What is the bug biting you to act? Without a clear answer to this question, it will be nearly impossible to build a viable business. But once you determine your driver, it becomes the jumping-off point for everything that follows as you become an entrepreneur.

In my experience, there are four main drivers that urge an individual toward becoming an entrepreneur: independence, wealth, recognition/ fame, and contribution.

Which is your driver? Which of these reasons is the primary one dictating your decision to consider beginning a business? You will likely find that you have a mixture of all of these, but it is important that you pinpoint your main driver by considering how far you would be willing to go and how much you would be willing to sacrifice to obtain each one. When you discover which of the four you would pursue with more vigor, intensity, and determination than you would the others, you've found your primary driver.

Independence is a driving factor for many entrepreneurs. They are motivated by the day when they can fire their boss and walk out of the office with the confidence that they possess the market knowledge and a quality product that will allow them to manage a business effectively, honestly, and profitably.

If you are seeking an opportunity to set your own terms of employment and to work by your own standards toward your own goals, then independence is probably your main driver—and that's one of the most exciting things about entrepreneurship. Excitement and thrills come with knowing that you are your own boss, president, CEO, supervisor, manager—whatever title you want to use. It is incredibly empowering, but more than that, it is incredibly freeing.

The fulfillment that comes with being one's own director, creatively and productively crafting and shaping a business, is a tremendous motivator for many people. A thriving, free-market capitalist system in which anyone can try to succeed by doing what he or she loves is one of the aspects of the American tradition that makes this country great; independence is an integral part of that tradition.

Wealth is also a great motivator. Unless you were lucky enough to be born as a trust-fund baby, chances are good that you have to work for a living. There is more to being driven by wealth than simply wanting a fat paycheck; however, if that's all you're after, there are far more secure means of achieving that goal.

If the desire to accrue wealth is your driver, it is probably because you have a business idea that you know has tremendous earning potential because it will meet a need or fill a niche better than anything else on the market right now.

There is no need to be ashamed if wealth is your driver. It has been the driver of nearly every great advancement that's ever been made—from the sixteenth-century explorers who circled the globe looking for gold, spices, and land to the ongoing competition between Microsoft, Apple, and the other computing giants who want to hold on to a significant corner of the market.

Some people act as if "profit" is a dirty word, as if the pursuit of making money as a small-business owner somehow makes you greedy, or that concern with the bottom line means you're a Scrooge. Nothing could be further from the truth. By generating wealth, you are providing for your own needs, for your family's needs, and—moving beyond your own immediate considerations—you are probably creating jobs in your community, as well.

Recognition and **fame** are reasons some enter the entrepreneurial life. If you have a solid product or service, you should take pride in that, and having your name associated with what you do demonstrates to your customers (and your employees) that you have confidence in your company.

Fame can be a tremendous motivator for someone who is tired of being counted as only a number in a company or as an average Joe without any real zeal for achievement. The desire to have your skills noticed can be a strong motivation, especially if you have felt underappreciated in your previous work. Recognition can bring a kind of validation in proving to the world that you are smart, savvy, and tough enough to succeed as a business owner.

The person driven in this way is also often seeking fulfillment—satisfaction from a job that exercises his or her unique talents and abilities in a manner that can bring respect. If this is what drives you, your competitive nature is going to love the thrill of the development, marketing, and service required to make it in the world of business ownership.

As long as you make sure that your self-worth is not dependent upon how well your company does, I would argue that it is actually healthy to foster a desire for recognition. Fame can bring respect and can open doors for opportunities to grow your business, expand your brand, or even start an entirely new venture.

Contribution is also an important driver. People who desire a sense of contribution feel compelled to give back to their community or to meet a basic need for people, animals, or the environment—any cause that promises to enrich lives or leave the world a better place.

Often, entrepreneurial-minded individuals who find themselves driven by a desire to contribute are drawn to the service industry or nonprofits. If this is you, you may find yourself in a bit of a quandary: Is it possible to operate a for-profit business like a nonprofit one, or vice versa? Absolutely.

True nonprofits depend largely upon grants, donations, and public funding to operate. You can create a business model that meets the same needs as a traditional nonprofit, but you can operate in such a way that it is not dependent on external funding. For example, a business that works with local governments to help place people in jobs or develop work skills can be self-supporting through the city's or county's payment for services. Likewise, it is entirely possible to run a profitable business dedicated to helping other local businesses go green.

Do not let the drive to be a social contributor scare you away from the prospect of starting your own business. The two certainly can coexist. Just recognize that your ultimate goals are probably going to be different from those of many of the other business owners in your area. That's simply because you have different drivers, and the drive to contribute can be the foundation of a financially successful business whose profits can be further invested in the community, doing even more good work.

Did any of these four drivers strike a chord with you? Keep in mind that your primary driver might change with time and circumstance. Personally, I've felt each one become my primary motivation at different points in my life. The key is recognizing where you are *right now* as you get ready to start building your business plan and making sure that you are honest in your assessment of yourself. Otherwise, your business and your life will arrive in the wrong place because the goal you pursued the most aggressively wasn't the one you really wanted.

If you are driven by fame, you may find that the desire to amass personal wealth has to become secondary as you take on gratis projects to get your name out there. If you are driven by independence, you may have to wait until you have a slightly higher bank account balance before you begin investing in charitable or socially conscious causes, simply because you are pursuing security first. But later, when your business is firmly established and you're ready to move to a new challenge, you might find your primary driver moving, too.

By determining the driver that best fits your current situation and mindset, you will be articulating authority over your circumstances. You are giving a label to the personal force that is bringing about this change in your life. That feeling of control over your decisions is a major factor in the success or failure of a business because it empowers you to call the shots and make the right business moves.

As we all know, there are a number of things that go into becoming successful and maintaining success. Additionally, the demarcation of having "arrived" can be different for each person. The point at which you feel you have made it is a very personal thing. But by staying mindful of the criteria by which you set your goals, you'll have a better sense of how to evaluate your progress as you move your business forward.

My advice is that you need to be aware of your *primary* motivation, the main one driving this decision. For me, as I got ready to launch my first venture, the driver was pretty simple: I was a fame and recognition guy. I had a competitive nature, and I wanted to prove that I could compete. As soon as I found a vehicle for my talents, I wanted to be in the thick of things, fighting for my place and for the acknowledgment of my innovation and leadership skills.

The next question you need to consider in creating your business plan is this: Where is your passion? What do you absolutely love doing? After identifying your motivation, this needs to be the other starting point for developing your company; because if your heart isn't in it, you'll have a much more difficult time finding the energy required to get your idea off the ground and running.

Take stock of your skills, interests, and hobbies. Do you find a common thread? Determine what you are naturally drawn to, and evaluate your strengths, whether or not you have formal training in the area. Do not be afraid to push around some of the boundaries and preconceived ideas that might be limiting how you view yourself and your talents.

For example, my girlfriend was starting to question the future of her career. She was a successful actress and model who appeared in several movies, television shows, and advertisements. She had a definite career established, but she wasn't loving it.

We discussed the importance of finding her driver—identifying the appeal of that one thing that would motivate her to go to all ends. It wasn't recognition. There are quick and easy ways to gain fame (especially in the world of Hollywood) that she was not willing pursue. It wasn't wealth. There were other profitable lines of work, but she was focused more on obtaining personal fulfillment and expression than on chasing a massive paycheck.

So I asked her a very basic question: What would you choose as a career if you were guaranteed a steady income for the rest of your life, provided

 That's how the human mind works—we create definitions and an identity for our-selves, and we don't always realize that we can shift within those stereotypes and still have fulfillment. When I say I'm a specific kind of entrepre-neur, that doesn't limit me because, as an entrepreneur, I can do anything.

that you pursued this one thing? She immediately answered that she would be an interior designer. She loved color, shape, texture, and lines—this was why she was drawn to modeling in the first place. She had a strong sense of the aesthetic and of what makes something visually interesting. She'd never been to design school, but she always found herself mentally arranging and rearranging interiors because of an innate artistic sense.

However, she'd always had a strict definition of what "artist" meant: palette and canvas, or clay and wheel. She didn't realize that her own interest in expression also made her an artist. To watch her start to redefine herself in those terms was exciting. She had an end in mind, which was that she wanted to create beauty to make an impact on people. Her performance vehicle could change from photography to acting to design, but what she was seeking was the same: she wanted to obtain the fulfillment from design by asserting creative control and professional independence over artistic drive.

That's how the human mind works—we create definitions and an identity for our-selves, and we don't always realize that we can shift within those stereotypes and still have fulfillment. When I say I'm a specific kind of entrepreneur, that doesn't limit me because, as an entrepreneur, I can do anything. As a high-technology entrepreneur, I have refined exactly the type of entrepreneur I am to the extent that I can pursue it to an end—or maybe I can move outside high technology if I want to own a restaurant or start a real estate company. Our perhaps I may want to use my skills with technology to revolutionize a non-tech-savvy industry.

But first, it's a question of identity, of a person taking a look at what he or she loves. I've heard speeches from a number of life coaches saying, "If money were no object, what would you really do?" It's pretty much the same question I asked my girlfriend, and I think it's a good way to break the issue down to its most basic element. You have to look at what gives you gratification.

I remember hearing a musician once say that if he lost the ability to sing, he would wish himself dead; without the ability to sing his notes, his life would be meaningless. That's an intense passion, but it's not the kind of passion that is likely to be turned into a profitable business. I wanted to tell that man that fulfillment through music isn't limited just to the good feeling that playing an instrument or singing can create in you, the musician. Don't play for the rush of the crowd; play for the person in the audience who will feel a rush as he listens to your song. Don't play for the applause; play for the emotional connection that your music will create in someone else. Find the vehicle behind the satisfaction, and make it your goal to share that, to impart that joy into someone else's life. *That's* the way to real professional gratification through your personal passion—and if one instrument breaks, you can always pick up another.

For me, the area that really sparked my interest was technology, but my passion for that field was multifaceted. I was driven by intellectual curiosity for the subject matter; however, I was also intrigued by its earning potential and by the fulfillment and reward that it brought to me as an outlet for creativity—and competition.

My first experience with computers was fueled by my troubled relationship with my father and my desire to see if I could deceive him. Early in middle school, when my dad's addictions were the worst and I was still living at home, I earned some terrible grades in school.

Rather than face the beating that I knew was inevitable, I watched the mailbox and pounced on the report card when it arrived. I knew that Dad wouldn't miss it by a day or two, so I went over to my neighbor Jeremy's house and asked to use his family's new computer. I spent a couple of days carefully recalculating my GPA—if a D changed to a B+, how would that change the numbers?—and counting every space and hard return line so that my fake report card would be identical to the real one. Methodically and precisely, we recreated that report card on the dot matrix printer, with better (but believable) grades. I had steamed the envelope open, so when the new report card was ready, I dropped it back in, glued the envelope carefully shut, and put it back in the mailbox. My parents never caught on, and I avoided another pounding.

I realize that is not, perhaps, the best story to introduce how I discovered my passion. But it's the honest truth—and I still have that report card. More than just pulling one over on my dad, though, that incident stayed with me for a long time because it was empowering. I felt that a computer gave me the opportunity to assert control over a bad situation.

From that point on, I'd watch my sister's dad Steve (we all have different parents) repair computers, which he did for a living, and I was captivated by the engineering of them. I was fascinated by movies like *War Games*, which showed how kids could hack other computers. That association stuck with me: computers equal power.

The forged report card.

Later, when I was solidly a juvenile delinquent, I got into shoplifting. It wasn't normal things that I'd steal, like candy or video games; I went into computer stores and "liberated" books on how to repair and restore computers. I read up on everything I could about the technical side of computers because it was empowering for me to have working knowledge of an emerging field.

One day when I was in juvenile hall (for the aforementioned shoplifting, among other things), I was sent into the computer room for a typing skills class. I realized quickly that I was one of the only people there who knew how to work the computer system. From then on, every time I was in the computer room, I would mess with the system. Sometimes I would shut it down or delete a few files because the prompts were so simple back then. Sometimes I was even asked by an oblivious instructor to fix the "problem" that was making the computers crash. It was such a thrill for me.

I talked about computers all the time, to the point that the first gift Robert Hunt (soon to be my stepfather) ever gave to me was a CD-ROM. It was his birthday gift to me because his computer was pretty old and slow, and with the way I constantly talked about programming, he figured I'd want something that I could use to maximize the performance of that antiquated system. It was with this background that I started eyeing the data center at Logix, which was my first real opportunity in the field of computers, and that allowed me to start climbing the ranks.

The first time I boarded a plane in my adult life was for a trip from Los Angeles to Minneapolis to discuss a piece of software that Logix was developing for Mystic Lake Hotel and Casino. I was nineteen years old and had limited real-world experience, but as I talked to the president and other executives of Mystic Lake about what we could do for them that our competitors weren't doing, I had a realization: I wasn't the guy getting the commission for the sale, but I was the guy they bought it from.

It was suddenly so clear. Not only did I realize that an obvious passion for my business helped close the sale, but beyond that, I recognized that I was the engineer behind the product. I could write the code, or I could oversee the code writing; I could do the sales, or I could manage the account. And that was when I knew that I wanted to be an entrepreneur. It was from that "Ah-ha!" moment that I started to formulate my business plan for 24/7 Tech, a 24-hour-a-day technical support service—my first business.

As you can see, our drivers and passions can come from wildly different sources; the key is to understand what they are and why. My girlfriend needed to realize that she gleaned the most satisfaction from creative work. Once she made that connection and could see herself as an artist, the possibilities available to her—as well as the precise one she most wanted to pursue—became much more apparent. She also found that her driver was independence. She loved the idea of having the control over building her own brand of design services, and even though she had not recognized it, it was this same drive for independence that had been steering her career choices all along.

I had a bit of a rockier path. Even when I was striving to avoid detection, be it faking that report card or "fixing" the computers in juvenile detention, I was still seeking recognition. That was my driver. I wanted the satisfaction of knowing that I had mastered a skill, and (as I started to realize later, while working for my stepfather) I wanted someone to take notice of that and be proud of me. As that recognition started to pour in, my own confidence in the field grew to the point that I knew I would be able to launch out on my own, chasing the field that had captured my attention.

Think about Anthony Hopkins's road to success. Before he was an established superstar, he acted in every production he could. He was on stage as much as possible—and often for scant pay, but he was driven by the love of what he did, and he was willing to sacrifice almost anything to pursue it. What would you go to any ends to pursue, as Anthony Hopkins did with acting? What grabs your interest and won't let go, despite the long hours, little pay, and constant obstacles in your path? What wakes you up at night and keeps you from going back to sleep because you can't stop thinking about it?

It comes back to the question with which we began: What do you desire most? Independence, wealth, fame and recognition, or a feeling of contribution? Which one would you sacrifice the most to obtain? And, taking that one step further, what do you love enough to use as your vehicle in chasing that dream?

To boil it all down to one simple sentence, you have to look at what gives you gratification, and you have to figure out why. Those two elements make up the foundation of your business plan, and your business plan must be in place before you can take the next step to truly becoming an entrepreneur. Figure out what's gotten you to this point and what's keeping you going. Find your driver and find your passion. Together, they will be the bedrock of all else that follows.

Think about it long and carefully. Be honest with yourself. Write down all of the various and possibly even conflicting motivations that you feel. Take stock of your skills, and do an interest inventory—don't allow yourself to be boxed in by a few narrow ideas based on what your work experience has brought you thus far. You may even find it helpful to talk to friends and family about talents they've noticed you possess, because they might view your skills in a different way that is broader than you'd allowed yourself to consider in the past.

But in the end, you have to trust your gut. Don't go with what sounds like the right answer or what you think other people expect of you. That's one of the most important things about having a successful company—in some way, your company's products are unique from the other products out there, which is why the discerning consumer will choose you. Do not get hung up on preconceived ideas. Let yourself really explore your drivers and passions, and when you feel comfortable with your grasp of both, that's when you'll be ready to move on to the next step.

CHAPTER 3

DEFINE YOUR ASSETS

Your next move may require you to be even more brutally honest than you were when determining your driver. You're going to have to take stock of the resources available to you, and that means more than just finances, though that's obviously a major component. Some of your most valuable resources take a less tangible shape, in the form of talents and skills, opportunities, networking, influence, mentors, references, and other related ideas.

I won't be able to cover all of the various possible assets, and every situation is different. But as we discuss how to go about taking inventory of them, you might want to keep a running list of resources and *potential* resources in your own sphere that might prove to be beneficial to developing, launching, and maintaining your business. Some of the ideas are very closely related, and you'll definitely notice some overlap both in my discussion and in your own lists, but I categorize each asset under a different heading for a reason, and I hope you'll see the reason for thinking of each one in its own way as we move forward.

Much of what we cover in this chapter will be developed in detail in subsequent chapters. Right now, I just want you to start paying attention to all the various areas of your professional life that will be the most helpful in developing your business, and I'll ask you to start thinking creatively about the various ways that they can be of assistance as you develop your plan.

Let's start with your most necessary asset: funding. The biggest fear of many entrepreneurs—and the biggest goal—is to raise venture capital; those who have done it know that it is swimming with sharks. If you understand how the game is played, your chances of having a successful company are much higher; but if you don't understand it, your successful company is not going to be your company for too long, because the sharks are going to figure out how to take it out of your hands. It happens all the time. Conversely, if you have a failed company, you may feel that it's in large part due to the viciousness of the funders—but they're going to say it's because of your bad management. Either way, you have a failed company, a failed reputation, and no credibility.

 **No entrepreneur should live comfortably in the first year of his or her business. If you're not uncomfortable, you're not putting enough of yourself into the company to give it a fair shot at success.**

Funding your business is a process that only succeeds if you are knowledgeable about how to structure the transaction, and if you are smart when choosing with whom you work. You must ensure that you throw in your lot with the right people who align with your values and philosophies, and who have the right intention with regard to their investment. But that's a lot easier said than done.

Whether your start-up needs $500 or $50 million to get off the ground, (believe it or not, many businesses, particularly home-based business, can be started for as low as $500) you need to conduct a thorough assessment of your finances. What do you have in the bank? What do you think you might be able, realistically, to raise from investors? What do you have to offer as collateral to potential investors? What might you be willing to offer? How much do you think you could borrow from the bank? How much are you *comfortable* borrowing? And finally, what is the minimum you and your family need to live on each month?

That last question is absolutely essential, because it will affect all of your other answers. You need to determine exactly how much—and how little—your family can afford each month for all the necessities such as mortgage or rent, bills, and food. Even build in the cost of health care if you are going to be without insurance or are paying for your own coverage. The best advice I can offer in this realm is to find the balance between meeting your needs while living sacrificially. No entrepreneur should live comfortably in the first year of his or her business. If you're not uncomfortable, you're not putting enough of yourself into the company to give it a fair shot at success. Familiarize yourself with this idea—it's going to come up a lot in later discussions.

In the last chapter, we already covered the importance of taking stock of your interests and skills when we discussed the steps to finding the things that drive you—your motivation and your passion. An exhaustive skills inventory is also an important part of defining your assets.

Is there an area where you have a great amount of knowledge, either thanks to hands-on experience in a prior job or through personal interest and study? Consider those skills carefully to determine if they really are strong enough to build a viable business with a quality product.

In his book *Outliers*, Malcolm Gladwell, the great writer and author, makes the point that it takes approximately 10,000 hours of training and practice to truly master a skill set at a professional level. Much like pilots have to log a certain number of flight hours to obtain their licenses, the number of technical hours you've amassed in perfecting your craft will make a difference in determining how fast your business gets off the ground.

Keep in mind, though, that this does not necessarily mean that you have to have a degree or extensive and formal classroom training in that area to succeed. Obviously, if you're hoping to start a business in the field of home health care, you'll need to have the training and credentials that allow you to practice that profession. But for many fields, it's not necessary to have spent countless hours working on the precise area you're now eyeing to turn commercial for you. Like my girlfriend who didn't hold a degree in interior design, her years of aesthetic studies, art classes, photographic work, and similar pursuits all contributed to the skill set that she could bring to interior designing. Make sure that you take into account related, if not identical, experience in your area of interest.

If you don't feel you have the requisite skills to accompany your talent or interest yet, then perhaps you should focus a little more time on developing them before you launch your business. In chapter 12, I will talk more about the importance of being a student of your field, but as you define your assets, your experience and knowledge will be important players in determining whether your talent is developed to the point that you can base a business on it.

Another asset to consider is the opportunities currently available to you. Within your skill set and interest sphere, are there any niches to fill? If you can identify a definite need for an area—there is no fabric or craft supply store within thirty miles, for example—you can have a clearer sense of how to tailor your plan to fill that hole. Similarly, there may already be a business in place, but perhaps it is currently up for sale. This is also an important type of opportunity to consider during this evaluation.

One of the most important elements in taking stock of your situation is a critical eye to determine whether there is anything right there, waiting for you to act. In some ways, it's doing reconnaissance, much like a covert military operation to scout out an area. A careful, detail-oriented examination of the exact field and area you're about to enter will help you make your decisions about when and how to act.

The best example I can offer from my own life of assessing opportunity comes from one of my earliest business ventures. One of my sisters was married to a man who owned a small Internet service provider that served their community. It was 2001, and there was a mix of nervousness from the dot-com bubble's recent implosion and optimism in the fact that the Internet itself was still a solid and reliable resource.

My brother-in-law got word of another small Internet company called SkyPipeline, which was coming up for sale. It was struggling, but because it was based in populous Santa Barbara, I could see right away that there was a definite opportunity for expansion. My previous experience enabled me to identify the company's main problem right away, and I could envision the most likely course of action to turn things around.

It was a tiny company, created with only about $20,000 in capital, and it served fewer than ten customers. Of course, you have to start somewhere with building your client base, but they were making less than $1,000 per month and were burning far more trying to provide service, maintenance, and repair. I recognized, however, that they had huge growth potential for their location and product.

I still owned 24/7 Tech, my technical support company, but I felt that this struggling little wireless company would be a great investment as a side business, and could maybe even grow into my primary company. Most of my money was already tied up in my established business, though, so I knew I would have to make some tough decisions if I felt that this opportunity really was the right one for me.

Opportunities are certainly an asset. Treat them as such while you look around and try to determine your best move into the world of ownership. It may be that your best opportunity is to create an entirely new business, but entrepreneurship is not necessarily creating a business from the ground up. There may be small companies out there that are ripe for purchase, restructuring, and rebranding. Keep your eyes open for any situation that might be a good one for you to act upon, and consider carefully how it may be something that fits—or could be made to fit—your professional passion.

In studying the possibilities out there, one of the best moves you can make is to network. Your ability to network is unquestionably an asset that should be taken into account.

Around the same time that I was looking at SkyPipeline, I was slated to make a presentation to a potential 24/7 Tech investor. King Lee was the ex-CEO of Quarterdeck, a large software company whose products we used daily. I knew he was a well-connected individual, and I convinced him to meet with me so I could pitch my business idea. At the end of my presentation, he remarked frankly, "Ryan, this thing that you were telling me about with wireless service— that has legs. Everything else I've heard I'm not interested in. Let me know if you ever decide to do the wireless thing."

That was the signal I needed to go forward. I knew that I would have one interested party, once the new company was up and running. But how could I get to that point? The key would be to see who else might want to invest in this company—but I found that raising capital was far more difficult than I had imagined. Time and again I was rejected by venture capitalists I spoke with because they didn't think it was a scalable model, or they felt there were too many competitors in the market, or they just didn't think it was a good business to invest in because it was already struggling. I believed in my vision for SkyPipeline, though, so I decided to pursue one other direction that had worked so far: I networked.

I knew of a successful angel investor in Santa Barbara named Pete Sutherland, who I thought might be interested in the potential of the company. I was able to book a meeting with Pete, wherein I presented him with my idea to purchase SkyPipeline, a plan that involved selling my share of 24/7 Tech. Pete was willing to help fund my business plan and to let me work with some accountants to get my finances in order, partly because I had demonstrated my willingness to reach out to other people for effective fund-raising, and partly because I was investing a huge portion of myself into the project. Pete's assistance enabled me to go forward with the purchase and helped the business grow rapidly, once I took over.

 **Networking is key because it can help bring about another asset worth considering: influence. Do you have connections to any individuals with significant sway—or does someone you know have those connections?**

My investment in 24/7 Tech was small—not much more than about $30,000—and combined with my savings, I was able to scrape together $20,000 to make an offer on SkyPipeline. Of course, I acted as if I had all the confidence and assets in the world, but writing out that check really did pain me because I knew I was going for broke. I had a mortgage and a car payment, and it was really a leap of faith.

But where networking really made a difference for me was when Pete stepped in and was willing to mentor me, to talk me through the negotiating process. Even though I started out with no home office, employees, camaraderie, or fancy logo, I had a solid plan and obvious confidence in myself and in the business that convinced others it was a solid investment. Pete explained to me that this ability to network was one of the most crucial elements in success. Business veterans already know that fact, but as a new kid starting out, this was an important lesson for me. And it paid off. Pete agreed to invest $75,000 to help get SkyPipeline off the ground, and then he agreed to help me lead a round of financing with other investors. And it was all because he saw that I was willing to reach out and do the legwork to meet people, make connections, and gain interest.

Networking is key because it can help bring about another asset worth considering: influence. Do you have connections to any individuals with significant sway—or does someone you know have those connections?

Once I had Pete's backing and I knew that another powerful business figure was interested (thanks to networking), their influence was able to help catch the attention of other potential investors. Influential individuals who believe in your product, who can endorse your company, or who can help to spread the word about your work are priceless.

Take stock of the most powerful and well-connected people in your circle. Whom could you reach out to? Make a list of these individuals, and keep those connections hot with the occasional note or checkup e-mail. Don't go overboard, but keep yourself in their mind's eye. These connections are the most valuable assets in your arsenal.

My networking with Pete proved to be valuable because he was also an influential individual. I bought SkyPipeline in July of 2001 and immediately started meeting with potential investors and clients to whom Pete had introduced me. With $75,000 in the bank—the first half of his investment money—I already had my eye on a bigger goal to expand the company right away.

And then September 11 happened.

That summer, the Dow had reached its all-time high. The NASDAQ had also been doing extremely well and was just starting to slow. But after the terrorist attacks, the market plummeted and investors lost fortunes. Here I was, one month into a business, and the market was the most volatile it had been in years. All my leads dried up. All my potential investors pulled out for more secure investments, nervous that telecom was too edgy.

I knew it was necessary to put Pete's influence to work or risk total failure. I called him up and explained to him that if we couldn't get any more backers— and soon—he'd lose the $75,000 he'd already put into the business. A smart man and a shrewd investor, he went to work with me, reaching out to various people and companies to give our sales pitch. By December of that same year, we'd closed $415,000 worth of financing, and the company had an exponentially larger clientele than when I'd started. Networking and influence can be very, very powerful tools.

I learned that lesson again as we moved forward into 2002, when I got a call from a man named Fred Warren, who had a ranch in Santa Ynez Valley, not far from Michael Jackson's Neverland estate. It was a rural area with thousands of acres of open land, but it was also a community with a lot of wealth. Fred wanted our service, and because my company was operating in the area, he gave me a call to see if SkyPipeline could handle the job.

Of course I was willing to take any contract I could, but I also realized that the cost of providing service just to Fred's ranch was probably not going to be a wise move, financially speaking.

I had no idea who this individual was, but he said he'd be willing to pay the $5,000 required to set up a tower facing his property, so I offered to meet with him to discuss the details and tell him more about our company—to see if it was an arrangement we could both benefit from. In the meantime, I Googled him and learned that he was the founder of Brentwood Associates—and one of the world's most-renowned venture capitalists.

We sat down at our meeting, and I pitched my business to him, explaining about the funding I did have and the potential investors I had lined up. Fred looked at me and said, "You need more than another $415,000. You need another million, and I'd like to participate with you." Suddenly, I had a new business partner with more influence, clout, and capital than I could have ever imagined.

Now obviously, an experience like I just described is atypical. But it doesn't change the fact that a few well-situated investors can give your business a huge advantage—especially in its early stages. As you consider your assets, do not be shy about counting the connections of people you know as possibilities. Don't be afraid to reach out to people who can help you. It's how the business world works, and you need to be ready to jump into the fray.

However, you should never slip into the trap of regarding powerful and well-connected people only as a means to financing. Successful business leaders have a wealth of knowledge and experience from which you can learn, and you should genuinely try to get to know them as individuals.

I will discuss the importance of mentors further in chapter 8, but it is important to acknowledge them here as you prepare to scrutinize all the assets available to you. If there are any successful entrepreneurs with whom you could speak about challenges and unforeseen obstacles, they are a great resource. Even if the individual isn't in your field, he or she has a set of experiences from which you can learn a great deal.

And don't limit yourself to entrepreneurs. Make note of any people you look to for guidance, reassurance, or solid advice; these names are important additions to your arsenal of assets. Their support, suggestions, and even criticism can be among the most important resources for your business.

Seek out those who are in your circle and from whom you can learn. Note those whom you can reach out to personally, such as successful business leaders in your family, your church, or your community. Make an appointment to speak one-on-one with a business professor from a nearby college. Take stock of *any* possible mentoring experience that could allow you to ask questions and seek advice from someone who has been where you are.

Sometimes one mentor can lead you to another, as well. When SkyPipeline started to expand rapidly following Fred Warren's investment, he put me in touch with Todd Goergen, whose family owned a number of large and diverse companies, such as Sterno, PartyLite Candles, and Miles Kimball. At the time, the Goergen family's businesses were doing about $2 billion a year in sales, and Fred knew that they were some of the smartest business leaders out there. With Fred on board as part of the company to help advise me in decision making, he also directed me toward people like Todd, who he felt could help me grow as an entrepreneur. I learned a lot as I watched how they systematically leveraged people in the boardroom and managed their influence for the good of the company. Personal connections that open the door to other mentors can be a tremendous boon to both the breadth and depth of your professional knowledge.

But don't just look for in-person mentors. You should also hunt continually for the iconic figures of business whose branding, marketing, and business style you admire. When I started reading *Forbes*, *Fortune*, *Success*, and other business magazines, I started making notes of the figures whose stories intrigued me and whose practices I wanted to emulate. I started seeking out more and more information on these people, allowing their stories, their skills, and their trades to mentor me. Their experiences crafted me into a better businessman because I was able to learn from both their triumphs and their mistakes.

Figures like Paul Allen, Steve Jobs, Marc Andreessen, Larry Ellison, Warren Buffett—these were my Michael Jordans and Brett Favres. While other guys I knew were pouring over sports statistics, I was glued to the financial reports, trying to glean every little lesson I could from these icons. That's not to say that there aren't business lessons you can learn from sports, though. Figures like John Wooden—paragons of integrity and effective team management—can be wonderful sources of inspiration. Figure out whom you respect and want to be like in your own life, and then pour yourself into studying those people. Write them to ask for a mentoring meeting. You never know—you just might get lucky!

Never underestimate the value of mentors in your life, both personally and professionally. They are an indispensable resource and one of your most valuable assets. Allowing yourself to be mentored both in person and by proxy will open you up to wisdom, know-how, and life lessons that can benefit your company by putting you years ahead of the learning curve.

Hand-in-hand with mentorship, you should also be aware of the importance of strong references. A solid set of references from well-respected individuals

Ryan with one of his mentors, Coach John Wooden.

can create a sense of stability, familiarity, and even legitimacy with prospective investors and clients. Your references are assets.

Don't be afraid to ask one of the mentors with whom you have had personal contact if he or she would be willing to be listed as a reference for you. This lets your mentors know that you respect their reputation and that you're actively involved in building and growing your company—which can possibly lead to networking opportunities. You could even go a step further and ask your mentors to write you a letter of recommendation that you can keep on file. This will not only help build the credibility of your business, but it can also be an important confidence builder for you as the company owner.

I do want to offer a word of caution here, though: never enter a mentor/mentee relationship because of what you think the other person can do for you beyond teaching. Of course, there might be networking possibilities down the road, and a meeting like this may very well get you into that individual's Rolodex, but you should never treat the meeting as such. Seasoned professionals can quickly spot the difference between someone who is genuinely there to learn, and someone who is just hoping for a shortcut to some potential leads. When you determine exactly what your assets are in the realms of mentoring and recommendation, make sure that you are counting the people you are genuinely seeking to learn from and whom you hope to have vouch for you—don't let ambition get in the way of the important lessons your mentor is seeking to share.

There are many more possible categories of assets to discuss. For example, you must determine the specialized equipment you may need, what you already have, what you can buy and for how much, and what the cost will be to store and maintain it all. And then there is the question of facilities: Will you be able to work from your home, at least at first, or are you going to need a brick-and-mortar location on the day you open your doors? These questions are all dependent upon the individual needs of your business and your vision for it.

I hope that the ideas presented in this chapter have given you a solid base to start your own asset inventory and have sparked ideas about assets you might not have considered as such previously. This process is not a quick one to be completed in just a few hours or days. Please take the time to consider, seriously and methodically, all of the possible types of assets you will need to take stock of, as well as the items and people who will fit under each heading.

You need to strike a balance between being realistic and allowing yourself to think big. As you make your lists, it will be helpful to create a kind of ranking system to rate how certain or secure an asset is. For example, if you have $15,000 in the bank but anticipate that you might be able to secure a $20,000 small business loan, make a note of that. Both are assets, but one is certain and the other is a realistic—but as of yet, unattained—goal. Likewise, if your father ran his own business for years, it is probably pretty certain that you'll be able to establish a mentoring relationship with him. But if there is a famous studio photographer you admire but who is notoriously difficult to book, it may not be as easy to schedule a meeting with her. That doesn't mean you should leave her off your list; it just means that you need to be aware of your solid connections, your possibilities, and your "would-love-to-haves." There are several people who once were on my would-love-to-have list, whom I now proudly call personal mentors. Making this list will give you a pool of assets to count on and a pool to pursue. That's the way business operates, too—you have your sure bets and the leads you're going after.

The most important thing is that you are thorough, organized, and honest with yourself as you go through this self-audit. A clear sense of where you *currently* stand, where you think you *could* stand, and where you one day *hope* to stand is key in preparing your business plan and approach to your own personal style of entrepreneurship.

CHAPTER 4

TOLERANCE FOR RISK

Maybe you have a pink slip in hand, your two weeks' severance pay in the bank, and you're ready to forget the employee world once and for all as you prepare to become your own boss. Or maybe you have a solid and reliable job, but you are seriously contemplating stepping out on your own. You've figured out what drives you and what your passion is, and you're evaluating the various assets available to you. The prospect of starting your own business sounds exciting, promising, and liberating—you're eager to get started. Now is the point where you have to start considering the less glamorous side of entrepreneurship. You need to determine how averse you are to risk.

Some people thrive on the thrill ride of risk; some people collapse under the strain of it.

Others neither relish nor shrink from it, but simply accept it as a necessary part of their business plan. Which one are you?

The fact is that entrepreneurship isn't for everyone. It is necessary to have a firm grasp on your tolerance for risk before you can even hope to make a jump into business. Your ability to manage living on the edge financially for at least a year in many ways is what will make or break your business.

The next two chapters are going to discuss the issues that are the most crucial for determining whether you're cut out for this: how far are you willing to go, and what are you willing to lose to possess your own business? It's not so much a question of strength as it is a question of temperament. Is your personality one that can adequately deal with the various unpredictable and constantly changing unknowns that go along with business ownership?

 **The risks are everywhere—that's the reality of business ownership. For every spending decision you make, there's another risk that it might not be the best one. Are you willing to take each of these necessary risks to turn this goal into a reality?**

In our last chapter, we discussed the need to define your assets. Now, you have to assess your tolerance for risk—and the tolerance of others around you.

Security is not part of the entrepreneur's lifestyle for at least the first full year. You have to accept that fact before you can even hope to have a realistic business plan. Any commercial you see on TV or any claim you hear from someone making a pitch saying, "I made X dollars in my very first month working from home!" is likely either a gross exaggeration or testimony from a person with significant skill and relevant experience. Security is not going to be part of the game for quite some time. Are you ready and willing to deal with that?

Once again, I need to stress the importance of being totally and completely honest with yourself. You have to be frank about who you really are and not just who you want to be or how you want to be seen by others. It's a good thing to show a lot of confidence and toughness when you're meeting with potential investors, but when you're considering whether this world is right for you, you can't put on a show for yourself. You have to be as brutally honest as possible.

It's really not about strong versus weak or tough versus soft. This is about the way you look at the world and the way your body and mind process stressful situations. If you know that you are not someone who performs well in high-pressure situations, you need to seriously question whether entrepreneurship is the right move for you.

First, you'll need to consider what is at risk. Your personal finances will definitely be at risk because you'll be investing a good amount of those into starting your business. Your home or car may be at risk if you use them as collateral for a bank loan. Luxury items, such as a boat, might be at risk if you find you need to sell them to raise capital. Your lifestyle will certainly be at risk as you make sacrifices such as the ones we will discuss in chapter 5.

But there is more at risk than just your material possessions. Your sense of security will be at risk as you wait on deals to come through. Your peace of mind will be at risk as you stress about establishing a clientele or securing enough investors to grow the company to keep up with the market. And of course, if it all falls through, you risk the disappointment and heartache of a failed business.

The risks are everywhere—that's the reality of business ownership. You will have to take daily risks to get things moving as you meet with investors and clients, and even as you reach out to mentors. There is always a risk of their turning you down. Can you handle that? For every spending decision you make, there's another risk that it might not be the best one. Are you willing to take each of these necessary risks to turn this goal into a reality?

It's essential to remember, however, that risk taking is not the same as being reckless. You may be someone who tends to be fairly cautious in your decisions and conservative with your plans. That doesn't mean you're not equipped to handle the pressures of entrepreneurship. In fact, you might be ideally suited for it.

People often confuse high risk tolerance with a willingness to fly off the handle with spur-of-the-moment choices that reflect little market research and no serious consideration for the current situation of the company. They are not the same thing at all. Reckless people rarely succeed in this field because they don't properly invest the time and energy required to make informed decisions, risky though the decisions might be.

If you are someone who craves risk for the sake of an adrenaline rush, go skydiving. If you're someone who can put up with risk as the cost of doing business, then you're an entrepreneurial-minded individual.

Consider each of the following situations:

- You have enough in the bank to take care of three months' worth of expenses, but no more. Sales have dried up, and it looks like you'll barely be able to cover operating expenses this month. Can you handle it?

- Your bank account has reached zero. You have some leads but no signed deals, and the end of the month is rapidly approaching. Can you handle it?

- Your balance is overdrawn, the credit card companies are calling you demanding payment, your child has to have her tonsils out, the transmission just blew on your family's only car, five customers are clamoring for service on their accounts, and your last investment pitch was just soundly rejected. Can you handle it?

At what point would you curl up into a ball on the floor? Which scenario would be the one during which you would finally decide it was all too much for you? Where is the line you'd draw, where you just couldn't find it within yourself to pick up the phone one more time and start working your way down a list of prospective clients?

There are degrees of discomfort, and everyone has a different breaking point. Each person has a different line over which he or she will choose to throw in the towel rather than go any further. But if you want to be an entrepreneur, there is no choice. You always have to be willing to make that next call, go present that next pitch, and work to close that next deal. If you know that you have it in you to go out and sell, even in the toughest of circumstances, then you've probably got the right personality, temperament, mindset, and confidence to make it as a business owner. If not, you may want to reconsider your decision, or at least your approach.

There are a number of entrances into the world of entrepreneurship—you don't have to jump into it immediately, or even all at once. Some people can't sleep at night without knowing that they have six months of living expenses in the bank. This is admirable and responsible. However, if this is your comfort level, you might not be ready to become an entrepreneur. You may need to start saving money now to have that security cushion, with the goal that in one year you'll be ready to strike out on your own. You may even want to take out a second job during this time frame, knowing that the extra income is going to support your goals of business ownership and that the current sacrifice will lessen the risk to some extent.

As I mentioned in the previous chapter, there are many businesses that can be started with very low risk and built from home while you save up to become a full-time entrepreneur. I don't recommend getting a second job to most of the entrepreneurs I work with, but I do suggest they start a business from home so they can earn additional income, learn the ropes of entrepreneurship, take advantage of the tax benefits, and build a business with limited risk.

It might be better, too, for you to keep two accounts during those twelve months— one for living expenses once you start your own business, and one as your business fund. If you know that you tend to be a more cautious and risk-averse individual, then you'll probably want to make sure that you have a solid savings account—not only for your family but also to hold a nice chunk of change for launching your business when the time is right. It can take quite a while to get the right investors interested when you're first starting out, so having in place a large amount of the initial start-up cost might be really important for your peace of mind.

Maybe during this time you can begin to acquire the necessary equipment, establish your Web site, or research the necessary paperwork and tax laws regarding the kind of company you'd like to establish. By taking these small but essential steps, you can help to spread out the cost and the legwork over a longer stretch of time so that the impact isn't quite so jarring, and the financial burden of the start-up cost doesn't sock you all at once. A more cautious, slow approach might lessen the financial risk so you can keep your family's savings account intact and help ease the feeling of extreme risk that might be holding you back.

The same thing is true if you're someone who is not comfortable with owing large amounts of money. Though they are a great tool for many people, small-business loans might not be the best route for you because of the looming knowledge that payments are going to come due and interest will be accruing. If that's how you feel about the matter, that's great—it's healthy to want to live debt free. Unfortunately, that's not an option for most first-time entrepreneurs. If you know you want to be an entrepreneur but you aren't comfortable having a great deal of debt, you may need to temper your approach and make a more cautious entrance after a longer preparatory period.

When I started SkyPipeline I had to put a lot of expenses on my credit cards. I personally guaranteed hundreds of thousands of dollars in loans and had to live off the company. This technique for starting a business is often called bootstrapping. I remember saying to myself, "If this doesn't work, I'm ruined." Leveraging yourself as I did is not for the security-driven, employee-minded person, because I recall having to make several difficult personal decisions to keep the business alive. I can look back now and say it was all worth it; however, I will never forget the feeling of financial uncertainty that haunted me along the way. My advice to all entrepreneurs is to try to avoid personal guarantees. I've learned this lesson the hard way.

In the end, though, you need to be aware that nothing will ever remove all the risk. No amount of preparation—personal, financial, or otherwise—will completely lift the uncertainty that surrounds business ownership. There is no fail-safe approach to being an entrepreneur, which is why it is so important to do this self-assessment before you get into the thick of things.

 **In the end, though, you need to remember that there is risk in everything. The fact that you've managed to live this long and accomplish as much as you have demonstrates that you have at least some level of risk tolerance.**

The most important thing is that you know what you're getting into. I've been in a scenario just like each of those listed above. Each is scary in its own way, but you have to know how far you can go before you break. When will the stress and the pressure become too much for you? What is the point at which you will no longer be able to function? As a business owner, you may get close to that line, but you have to make sure you never cross it. You must not allow the challenges, pitfalls, and risks of your business to destroy you.

The risks are high, and you might be ready to take them on, but the other thing you have to consider is the risk tolerance of the other people in your life. Who else is depending on you, and how much risk can he or she tolerate?

You will likely need to find a solid answer to a number of questions: What other needs exist in your life right now? If you're married, what is your spouse's employment situation? Will he or she be working in this business alongside you, or does your spouse have another job that will be supplying income as you pursue your own business? Do you have any children who will be getting ready to head off to college soon, or who may have special needs? How might these circumstances change your risk tolerance? What about elderly parents, either within your household or in assisted living—do you provide any support for them? Might you need to in the next few years?

These are all serious issues you need to evaluate thoroughly before determining your own risk-aversity profile. However, you must also assess the risk-aversity profile of your main partner, be it your spouse, fiancée, or significant other. Where is his or her risk threshold in comparison with yours? You will need to sit down with your partner and discuss this issue openly. If you feel confident that you can take on a business, where is your partner's breaking point? At what point will he or she decide not to live with the uncertainty and the sacrifice anymore?

You may be able to weather the storm, but if your partner can't—if your partner craves security over any of the entrepreneurial drivers of independence, wealth, recognition/fame, or contribution—then you may need to rethink your plan. Perhaps you can reach an agreement of a prearranged stopping point at which you will both agree that enough is enough. You may be considering this business move to provide your family with a better life, which is totally admirable. If you are lucky and your family is fully supportive of the risk, you're going to be starting out in a great place with a solid support system in place. But if they aren't on board with your plan and don't share the same level of risk tolerance as you, your work on their behalf may all be in vain.

I'm not speaking empty warnings; I know firsthand that this can happen because I lost a family over this same issue. A number of years ago, my wife decided that the continual uncertainty and risk taking didn't fit her need for certainty. As a result, we divorced. You have to make sure that your family is supportive of the work you are doing and the lengths to which you will have to go to get your company on its feet. Otherwise, the discord that can result is a risk you'll have to consider as well.

In the end, though, you need to remember that there is risk in everything. There is a risk that your current company could move or downsize. There is a risk that management could change, or you could be asked to take a pay cut. There is even a risk that your personal circumstances could change in the future, making the possibility of starting a business less feasible than it is now. There is a risk attached to everything in life, and the fact that you've managed to live this long and accomplish as much as you have demonstrates that you have at least some level of risk tolerance.

There is risk in making the move to start your own business, but there is also risk in not acting. Don't let fear stop you from doing what you feel driven to do. Know what you're getting into and be prepared for the challenges it will bring, but you shouldn't let the fear of uncertainty paralyze you in indecision. Take control of your circumstances by deciding to act, in whatever capacity that might be.

Martin Luther King Jr. once said, "Most men die at 21; we just don't bury them until they're 60 or 70." Don't be someone who lives a life of excuses instead of action. Discern your tolerance for risk, and start working toward your goal. If your tolerance is high, that probably means you're in a good place to go forward with your business plan. If your tolerance is low, you should probably wait a little while longer and build up more of a security cushion.

Then again, maybe time is a luxury you don't have. Maybe you're out of work now, and even though the thought of taking risks ties up your stomach into knots, you're willing to do whatever it takes to make this opportunity work for you and for your family. If that's the case, just remember that the risks can be huge, but so can the rewards. If you are willing to accept the uncertainty for the sake of your goals, then you are ready to move forward. Entrepreneurship is not for everyone, but if you have nothing to lose, then why not get started?

CHAPTER 5

PREPARE FOR SACRIFICE

C losely related to your tolerance for risk is your willingness to sacrifice.

You not only need the ability to stomach a large amount of uncertainty in your daily life, but you also need to be willing to pare down to a minimal existence for as long as it takes to reach a point of sustainability with your company—which means at the very least a year or more. You have to determine just how uncomfortable you can possibly stand to be, not only forfeiting luxury items or little indulgences, but also forgoing physical comfort. You need to consider this seriously because without a willingness to sacrifice, you are never going to achieve your business goals.

Sacrifice is a word we tend to hear a lot about from politicians, but it's not something that most of us really keep in the forefront of our minds every day. However, that is going to change when you enter the world of entrepreneurship. "Sacrifice" is going to be echoing in your head continually as you make decisions regarding what you can afford, what you need, and what you're going to have to plan for.

There are several steps of sacrifice that you're going to have to take—starting with how you think about money in your personal life—even before you formulate your business plan.

I think it is apparent that most middle-class Americans are in a holding pattern of comfort. There is a desire to keep up appearances, and then appearances take on a semblance of reality to the people living them—and they feel that they have to borrow money to maintain a lifestyle that was phony in the first place.

When I was growing up in Southern California, wealth was all around me. Living as a normal middle-class kid until the age of thirteen—and living as a poor, teenage street kid for several years after that—everywhere I looked, I saw how the most successful business people, investors, and other professionals lived. That was what I wanted, and I was always curious about what it would take to get from where I was to where they were. What was different about the way they thought that opened them up to such success? What was their system?

By the time I was in my early twenties and back in the middle class, I had established a pattern of living that seemed very different from my neighbors' patterns. Whenever one of them earned a large amount of money, it seemed that a new car or a new boat would inevitably show up in the driveway. Maybe a woman would be flashing some new jewelry, or a man would be sporting a Rolex.

I fell into that trap more than once myself, purchasing a flashy new car that would stretch my budget or taking a lavish vacation with my raise or bonus. It feels good to spend money. I felt like I had finally attained the standard of living that I'd always wanted—until the bill came due. And then I realized the biggest difference between me and those people I had wanted so badly to emulate: they could afford to live in the manner I was only pretending to be able to afford. And why could they afford it? Because they had been smart with their funds early on, they could now reap the benefits.

 **You have to think of your money as an investment to be continually put toward something that will bring you a return and build wealth rather than as a tool to buy you the luxury items that only make it *appear* as if you are wealthy. You have to be willing to sacrifice to get beyond the illusion.**

Once I understood that, I quickly realized that my money would go a lot—*a lot*—further if I reinvested it instead of spending it. Once I started to channel it—but not toward personal comfort items or status-driven indulgences—I found that the returns would almost always generate even more capital. At first, I spent the money expanding my business. Later, I was able to use it to invest in other promising companies. And as the luxury-brand items were depreciating in my neighbors' driveways or closets, my money was continuing to grow. Investment over consumption—that has to be an entrepreneur's mantra.

There is nothing wrong with spending your own hard-earned money in whatever way you see fit. My stepfather always told me to take 5 percent of my gains and reward myself, but that's it! When you start making millions a year, you can have a lot of fun with 5 percent. As you will see later in chapter 11, I am a great proponent of incentive and rewards programs. However, the long-term future of our money depends on the choices we make for it today. Do you want to have a business that is stable, a community fixture able to weather the markets? Do you want to reach a point where, maybe someday, you could maintain a comfortable lifestyle simply from the interest paid from your capital? Then you need to be willing to make sacrifices now.

Don't fall into the unhealthy pattern of continually chasing the next cheapest offer for money from banks or credit card companies. That's how people land in debt, bankruptcy court, and the cycle of miserable employment. The entrepreneurial appetite is continually obstructed by the chase for cash. If your income-to-debt ratio is too high, you may never be able to launch your own business because the security of a guaranteed income will keep you tied to your current position (if you are still employed), even if the work is mind numbing. If you are currently out of work or anticipate being there soon, the same is true. If you are locked into debt and financing beyond your means, you will be desperate to take the first job that comes your way simply to be able to make your minimal payments. That will never allow you the freedom to do what you truly desire.

If you are part of the "comfort chase," as I like to call it, you have to start changing your mode of thinking long before you can hope to launch a feasible business. You have to think of your money as an investment to be continually put toward something that will bring you a return and build wealth rather than as a tool to buy you the luxury items that only make it *appear* as if you are wealthy. You have to be willing to sacrifice to get beyond the illusion.

Benjamin Franklin famously quipped, "A penny saved is a penny earned." Remember that, each time you decide not to spend and each time you choose not to pursue a new line of credit. You are investing in your future security and in the security of your business. The point of an investment, after all, is that a sacrifice with a bit of risk in the present will return dividends in the future.

If you really love what you want to pursue, necessary sacrifices will be much easier to deal with—which is why it is so important to have your driver and passion clearly identified before you start pursuing your dream.

But the fact is, the business world is built on more than just dreams. It's built on hard numbers and profit margins. And that's where the second level of sacrifice comes in. Once you have made the necessary changes to your way of thinking about money *before* your entrepreneurial leap, you have to be willing to maintain those changes—and possibly even take them to a new level—once your plans get rolling.

When you have external investors in your company, you have a duty to make them a return. An investor might say, "All right, you told me what you love and how you propose to build a business around that, but what I want to know is how you are going to fund this business to support yourself and your lifestyle." If you haven't considered the way you're going to live while getting your business off the ground, an investor is not going to be interested in anything else you have to say because it means you haven't thought through the situation thoroughly.

We will be discussing how to build a business plan in the next chapter, and the first thing you need to consider is where you fit into it. Whether you're starting a home-based business or launching the next Google, many potential entrepreneurs will forget their own needs in light of their vision for the company. Don't fall into that trap. You have to take into account not just how your business is going to survive, but how you and your family will as well. You want to formulate your business plan with you in it—as an employee or as a CEO—and you have to ask for what you need to live.

But . . .

Entrepreneurs who are asking for other people's money should not be asking for what they *want* to live on—neither their eventual salary goal nor an amount equal to their current lifestyle demands. An entrepreneur has to ask for what he or she *needs* to live—and that means preparing for sacrifices.

As an investor, I want a person who is going to sacrifice to get me a return on my investment. Consider an investment pitch that opens like this: "I want you to give me $500,000 for a year to fund my business, and I'm going to take $250,000 to live on." No potential investor would be willing to commit to such a plan. I know I would turn it down because in a plan like that, not enough of my money is put to use. If that's the case, then why should I want to invest at all? What is the incentive for the business owner to work harder if he or she is already living comfortably?

Now if the entrepreneur were to say: "My bare needs to live on and to pay for my children's school, my mortgage, and all my bills are $75,000 a year. I need to earn that, and I need to earn more than that to be comfortable and have security," then I would be more likely to listen. We could work out a plan where I could tell him or her, "Maybe there's a way that if you hit your targets, I'll give you $70,000 and another $70,000 if you exceed your targets."

Too often, I meet entrepreneurs who are there to negotiate, and they misread my words when I say: "When you are looking for other people's money, tell people what you *need* versus what you *want*." You should never say, "Here's what I want" to an investor unless you're in a position of strength—you have a business that's strong, profitable, growing, and in demand. Unless all of those pieces are already in place and your company is thriving, asking for funds that will support a lifestyle of ease rather than tenacious pursuit of business is likely to come across to an investor as confident, cocky, and too risky.

When I put my money into a new business, I expect the owner to be uncomfortable for at least the first year. To me, if I cannot tell that the individual is willing to give up a lot of his or her comforts, I do not have confidence that my money is going to be stretched to its most efficient use, which means that my investment is not being maximized.

I've been there plenty of times. I know what it takes to get a business on its feet—and I know that you have to stay hungry for the next sale in order to pour the right kind of energy into your development in the early stages. If you're not uncomfortable, you're not going to be working as hard to create a superior product and to pursue clientele.

Take a look at your estimated start-up cost, then divide that number in half. Could you make it work on that amount? Divide it in half again. How about now? Those are the numbers you need to be considering when you anticipate your standard of living. When the available resources are greatly reduced so that you're in survival mode rather than surplus mode, it's amazing how quickly items that seemed to be necessities suddenly become expendable. Your essentials shift when your priorities do.

Repeat this same halving of capital with your estimated monthly budget needs. Could you make the business survive—could you survive—on an amount half or even a quarter of what you initially projected? If you find yourself facing that reality, what will you be willing to sacrifice in terms of your business plan and your personal life to keep the company afloat? The answer to that question should be "Whatever it takes, up to everything I have."

You have to be ready to make the company your priority over personal comfort, and you must demonstrate that to potential investors; otherwise, you are not going to be taken seriously. That is not to say that you should be reckless, though. Make sure that you account for every necessary expense as you determine the amount of your capital dedicated to self-preservation. This will become the starting point for your business plan.

As with determining your tolerance for risk, it isn't just your own sacrifices that need to be taken into account. If you are married, your spouse should be prepared for that sacrifice. If you have children, they should be prepared, too. This is the next realm of sacrifice that you need to consider: family-wide sacrifice.

It is essential that your partner be in total agreement with your plans for personal sacrifice. Before each step of the preparation process—when you set out to establish better spending/investment patterns (if you haven't already) and as you prepare to write your business plan—it is advisable that you sit down together at each stage and discuss how uncomfortable you are willing to be in terms of your lifestyle. Establish a detailed budget on paper so there is no room for disagreement in the future when things get tougher than you might have predicted. That's not to say you will be able to avoid all disagreements, but you can certainly help keep them to a minimum if you establish, at the outset, a clear plan to which you both agree.

Once you have completed this discussion with your partner, you should also set aside some time to explain to your children what kind of changes you are anticipating. Perhaps they will have to pass on horseback riding lessons this summer, or they may have to play soccer with a local league rather than a travel team.

 **What will you be willing to sacrifice in terms of your business plan and your personal life to keep the company afloat? The answer to that question should be "Whatever it takes, up to everything I have."**

Whatever the case, it is important to make sure your family understands that these sacrifices are something that the whole family is facing and that the whole family will benefit from them. Depending on the age of the child, it might be necessary to reassure him or her that your family will not go hungry or become homeless. It is important to understand from the beginning that everyone is giving a little bit to achieve something better for the family down the road. In addition to making sure that your entire family is in agreement with the plan, this will also help establish smart money behaviors for your children at an early age.

It's natural to be nervous, and even a little apprehensive, during major life changes like this, so make sure your spouse and your children feel your commitment to making it all work out. Take the time to assure them that your family unit won't change, but that everyone is going to need to step up their responsibilities to help pitch in. That could mean always checking that the lights are turned off when you leave a room to help save on electricity costs, or making sure that toys are picked up so that Mom and Dad have one less thing to worry about. Children should know that the little contributions they make are helping the family become better off in the long run.

That's because there is one more step of sacrifice that will be required, and that is your time.

I often jokingly explain entrepreneurship like this: you get to set your own hours—pick the seventeen hours of the day that are best for you, any seven days of the week. Of course, as exhausting as the hours can be, if you're doing what you love, it doesn't drain you in the way that the previously described Death Cycle does.

Even so, hard work is hard work, no matter what you're doing. You will need to sacrifice your spare time to research zoning laws, file license applications, deal with building permits, or tour retail space for lease. You have to be willing to sacrifice your leisure activities to improve your skills through reading books and enrolling in classes. You will need to research the trends and advances of your field, make new connections, and pursue the next sale—often all at once. Vacation time is not an option for a new entrepreneur; neither are weekends. Once your company is on firm footing, you'll have far more flexibility and far more freedom, but that doesn't happen overnight. It certainly doesn't happen within the first couple of months either, or even the first few years, for most.

Remember that your goals need to lay further down the road—at the five- or ten-year mark. That means you need to be willing to give up your free time now for the sake of having much more of it in the future. Without the sacrifice of personal time, your business will not have sufficient muscle and drive behind it to achieve a successful launch and build momentum.

 **If you're in the right place at the right time, it's because you worked hard and sacrificed to get there. Success isn't up to chance. It's about the choices we make—to act or not to act, to throw in the towel, or to get back in the ring.**

What it all comes down to in the end is the same refrain that is laced throughout this book: there is no secret by which you can bypass the hard work, sacrifice, headaches, and sweat equity required to establish and grow a business. The advice put forward in this chapter is not optional for an aspiring entrepreneur. It is essential. If you are not willing to make sacrifices, you will not succeed with your business—plain and simple.

An unwillingness to sacrifice is the single reason the vast majority of Americans never act on their dreams of striking out on their own. Most people are too tied to the moment to be willing to give up some of their present comforts, despite the potential payoff both financially and in quality of life. Most people lack the gumption to pursue a dream. Call it fear, call it a lack of vision, call it laziness—the point is that most people ultimately decide that they don't want to take the gamble.

But it's not a gamble—not really. There is risk, of course, but entrepreneurs know that there is no such thing as luck. If you're in the right place at the right time, it's because you worked hard and sacrificed to get there. Success isn't up to chance. It's up to your personal dedication to seeing through the necessary actions. It's about the choices we make—to act or not to act, to throw in the towel or to get back in the ring.

For example, if you want to open a hair salon, there are countless resources out there to get you started. The first action you need to take is to buy one of Paul Mitchell's numerous books and read it from cover to cover. Make notes. Formulate a list of questions. Look up the publisher's phone number, and ask how to contact the author. Of course, the odds are that you'll never hear back from Paul Mitchell, but if you spend a lot of time crafting your letter to reflect your serious interest in his philosophies and a genuine desire to put them into action, you'll increase your chances of receiving a response. But you have to take that first step and just *do it*.

If you encounter a number of obstacles while trying to set up your business, do not allow them to stop you. Rather than having a relaxing evening with a glass of wine or a weekend at the beach, you'll have to hit the pavement, knock on doors at city hall, and make however many phone calls and personal visits are necessary for the permit to go through or the lease terms to be settled.

Because such a degree of personal output is required, the majority of people retreat to the drudgery of their nine-to-five jobs that are creating wealth for someone else. That's the main difference between an entrepreneur and everyone else—the entrepreneur isn't afraid. He isn't afraid of the risk. She isn't afraid of the sacrifice. The entrepreneur isn't afraid to act.

It's natural to seek the path of least resistance, to seek out the simplest and most direct way to make something happen. The problem that most people face is that they change course if they hit any obstacle, or they simply give up if the goal isn't immediately attainable. Too many people believe in the power of intention. Yes, you need intention, but then you must have action to accompany it. Individuals can have all the intention in the world, but the reason that they are not successful is because they were unwilling to take the actions necessary to get there.

You have to be willing to let go of the comforts and luxuries to which you are clinging and allow yourself to face the harsh reality of uncertainties, personal risk, financial risk, and sacrifice. You have to act as if you have nothing to lose.

CHAPTER 6

BUILDING A BUSINESS PLAN

There is a lot of prep work required before you reach the point when you make a business plan. You first need to have done a lot of soul-searching, made detailed evaluations, had serious discussions with your family, and shifted your financial thinking to entrepreneurial thinking.

You now need to create your business on paper—the plan you've probably been composing in your head and on various scratch pads for a long time. It's time to transfer all of those notes and ideas into a formal, clear plan that will be the basis of your business's reality and the platform from which you reach out to potential investors and clients.

As with each previous step building up to this point, you will need to be prepared to think frankly, honestly, and realistically about your assets, finances, abilities, opportunities, energy, risk tolerance, and willingness to sacrifice. You should always want to think big, but be realistic about the steps you need to take to get there, because this is the part of your plan that makes your goals and aspirations official. It also sets the stage for the first impression your company will make in the marketplace.

The focus of this chapter is not to help you determine whether you should become an LLC or a C Corporation or to instruct you how to manage the patent process. There are great online resources, such as the US Small Business Association's Web site (www.sba.gov), to help walk you through that part of the process of formulating your business plan. These sites can steer you through the nuts and bolts of your industry's unique requirements as well as the general steps everyone must go through.

Instead, I want to focus on the mindset you will need to have as you enter into this phase of your business—what to consider, what to keep in the back of your mind, and what to watch out for as you bring your dream to life from page to pavement.

Before you begin creating spreadsheets and crunching numbers, though, I suggest that you begin your business plan by writing a purpose statement in which you outline the philosophies and vision that you want for the company you are creating. Post this where you can see it while you're working on your budgets and potential client lists. Keep a copy in your wallet so you have your purpose statement with you when you make spending decisions, and include an abridged version of it in your business plan. A tangible, visible reminder of your goals and ideals will help keep your focus and your mind in the right place as you create the plan that your business will follow.

 **With clarity of individual purpose, you will have clarity in your business; after all, you *are* your business. The perspective and direction a purpose statement can give you will be invaluable for the days when you want to give up, when you're questioning why you ever jumped into the world of entrepreneurship in the first place.**

In 2003, I sat down to create a purpose statement for my own entrepreneurial goals, and I created the following document:

- My purpose in life is to inspire the minds and actions of others in harmony with myself and with the minds of the people by whom I am inspired. I will lead others to their own personal greatness. I will mobilize an unstoppable army of like-minded individuals to achieve extraordinary results. I will help those in need and give the gift of an independent life to thousands of willing minds. I will give independence from abuse and self-destruction, independence from confusion, and independence from economic burdens. I will identify my unsuccessful beliefs and remove all beliefs that do not suit my purpose in life.

- In this pursuit, I will learn to identify GREATNESS in others with extreme accuracy, and I will hold myself accountable for all of my actions. I will operate with integrity, and I will seek feedback from others with an open mind for self-improvement.

- I will focus only on items I am deeply passionate about, items at which I can be the best in the world.

- I will set my mark as an individual who overcame great obstacles to achieve extraordinary success. I will help, both directly and indirectly, millions of people to do the same.

- I will measure my influence by the network of people I can draw upon for inspiration and economic creation.

As you can see from my personal purpose statement, it is nothing especially profound. It doesn't have to be. It just needs to be an honest declaration of the principles by which you intend to operate and the goals that you hope to achieve through your efforts. I have continued to revise, rewrite, and rework this original purpose statement as my situation has changed, but the core ideals and the vision remain the same. The irony is that in December of 2003, I had no idea what I was going to do. Looking at my purpose statement now, I can tell you that I am on the path toward achieving the results I dreamed of through the companies I am a part of. With clarity of individual purpose, you will have clarity in your business; after all, you *are* your business.

I urge you to take the time to complete this step before moving on to the more concrete parts of your business plan. The perspective and direction a purpose statement can give you will be invaluable for the days when you want to give up, when you're questioning why you ever jumped into the world of entrepreneurship in the first place.

Keeping your purpose statement in view at all times, you are now ready to start the actual plans for the business itself. One of the most important of these, and one of the earliest ones to focus on, is your company's name. I cannot emphasize enough how important it is to come up with the right name. Enlist family members and friends to help; bounce ideas off each other, and take note of which ones get positive reactions and which ones get groans.

When Don and I decided to write this book, I had no idea what to title it until Don mentioned that he had heard me say several times in an interview that the reason for my success was that I played as if I had nothing to lose. I immediately searched to see if NothingToLose.com was available and, as you can imagine, it wasn't. That didn't stop me. I looked up who owned it and that led to a company called DomainMarket.com, who had it for sale on their site for $35,000. I contacted them and, because they were inspired by the project, they agreed to sell me the URL for a reduced amount. It's still the most expensive domain name I've ever bought, but it was worth it to me to have that connection to my book. I tell you this because I want to stress that your business name is extremely important, and the brand equity that it creates may one day be your most valuable asset.

Just a few examples of clever names that I've encountered in the past few years include the coffeehouse chain Daily Grind, the Chinese food chain Wok 'n' Roll, a canine bakery named Fi-Dough, a cleaning company called Sweeping Changes—the list could go on and on. A creative title can make someone laugh, make someone look twice, make someone want to buy a shirt with the name emblazoned on it. Pictures of clever business signs are all over the Internet, and any exposure you get like that can be worth its weight in traditional print ads.

It's great if you have a fantastically clever or catchy name for your business, but it's just as important not to try to force a clever title. We've all rolled our eyes at a company whose name sounds a little ridiculous, is a lame pun, or is too far of a reach. You have to find something that fits and conveys the image you want your company to project. A high-end, sophisticated-sounding title might not work if you want your company to exhibit a casual, fun-loving atmosphere, such as a mobile pet-grooming business or someone who caters children's birthday parties. Similarly, a funny name might not be the best choice for a more serious or formal field, like accounting or wedding catering.

Make a list of all of the adjectives that you would like people to associate with your business, and then narrow it down to your top three or four. Using those words as your reference point, try to come up with names that match that image. You may need to dedicate a lot of time to finding just the right name that fits you and fits your business, since this will be the backbone of your brand.

This can be one of the most satisfying steps in the entire process, because once your company has a name, not only will you be able to use that title on all of the legal paperwork, but it can also help you think of your business in a solid, this-is-really-going-to-happen kind of way. A lot like selecting a name for an unborn baby, finally settling on a name for your business can really help make the reality seem more, well, *reality*. It can help you to wrap your brain around the excitement and the grandness of the undertaking you're about to face.

As you pore over names and sort through options in the back of your mind, you should also start on the practical side of the business plan by compiling a comprehensive list of funding sources. Looking back at what you listed during the phase of evaluating your assets, you should now begin figuring out how to tailor your plan to catch investors' interest. You shouldn't change your fundamental product, of course, but you need consider what it is that is going to make your business plan stand out from the thousands of other ones that cross investors' desks each day. What is your niche in the market? What need are you filling that no one else is? What can you do better than anyone else?

This uniqueness or "Wow!" factor is going to be a very important part of your business plan as well. Every time I am on television talking about entrepreneurship, I inevitably end up with about a hundred business plans sent to me by viewers. Of these plans, the entrepreneurs to whom I give an interview are, first and foremost, the ones whose plans fit my interests.

My experience is in technology. From computer and communication technology to nutritional technology, I am interested in providing more advanced services and more finely tuned goods than are currently available. Because this is the area I know, understand, and specialize in, I am naturally going to gravitate toward plans in line with those fields.

That's not to say you can't include other potential investors on your list who are outside your field, or whose connection to it might be a little looser; it just might be helpful to rank potential investors in terms of the degree to which you consider their aims and objectives similar to yours when you create your plan.

A good way to think about finding your business's unique place in the market is to look at what researchers call game theory. If two people are locked in a struggle to earn a prize, so long as the other person gives up first, what will each one do to get ahead?

The most common hypothetical scenario is that of two people who are tied together at the ankles and teetering at the edge of a cliff. The first one to back down loses. If one person starts jumping around or kicking his legs over the edge, the other person is likely to give up sooner—even if it means forfeiting the prize—because he is becoming too nervous. The person who did the jumping around held what is referred to as the "dominant strategy." That is, he took some risks and did something unusual to force his opponent to surrender.

 **Find what it is that you do better than anyone else, and make that the focus of your business plan. Making this kind of distinction for your business not only will help you with investors but also will give your business an organized mission that can help build your brand and your reputation in the community.**

In many ways, the business world is very similar. Most businesses are content to stay right at the edge of the cliff, barely breathing and praying the wind doesn't pick up to send them hurtling off the edge. In other words, they are passively trying to win. If you are willing to enter the contest with a dominant strategy, the difference of your approach to theirs is what will ultimately make you successful. Trying something that isn't being done can be risky, but it can also distinguish you in a way that leads to greater gains.

That dominant strategy is what you should be hammering out as you formulate your business plan. The unique offerings or unusual approach you take when meeting a need or solving a problem should be your focus. That should be the reason you are starting this entire venture. No one is interested in another company that does the exact same thing as everyone else—you'll just flood the market. Consider what it is that makes you unique, and explore why that unique-ness is so valuable. That will be one of your greatest strengths, so play to it!

When I was first launching SkyPipeline, it was a challenge to establish our place in the market. It was Southern California, and the tech bubble was still going strong, so there were many broadband service providers growing and competing for the same clientele. I started my company without a fully developed business plan—the numbers were all there, but I hadn't realized the importance of thinking about emphasizing our differentiation from every other company out there.

Finally, in one investment pitch, the venture capitalist asked me why he should choose my company to invest in over any of the dozens of other plans on his desk. I took a risk, a gamble—I picked up the phone and asked him to call our company's number. I promised him that, as a broadband wireless company, we would always have someone there to answer the phones promptly, and at a call center that was not located halfway around the world. It was a cold call. My staff had no idea I would be phoning the center, and I held my breath and hoped that my employees would represent our company well. Sure enough, the phone rang, a live person answered, my investor was impressed, and we got the capital to keep our business growing. Our greatest differentiation was in our customer service, and that's exactly what we focused on.

Find what it is that you do better than anyone else, and make that the focus of your business plan. I had been wasting time pitching other services and features ahead of our guaranteed quick-response policy. What I should have been concentrating on was the fact that we bypassed all of the usual frustrations of trying to get decent tech support and provided a faster and more reliable service than our competitors did. Making this kind of distinction for your business not only will help you with investors but also will give your business an organized mission that can help build your brand and your reputation in the community.

Then, of course, there are the hard numbers and budgeting proposals, which are probably what most people think of when they imagine drawing up a business plan.

You will need to account for all start-up costs, including any licensing fees, certifications, equipment purchases, employee salaries, and retail or office space required to open the doors to your business. I cannot offer specific advice as to the needs or vision of each individual company. I will urge you, however, to do your research through books, magazines, and online sources, and by interviewing other entrepreneurs to make sure you have as full and complete a picture as possible for the needs of your business. And, as I mentioned in chapter 5, you should have a contingency plan in place in case you find you have to operate on far less than your projected amount.

The start-up costs will vary a great deal from person to person and business to business, just as day-to-day operational costs will. For example, if you are planning to open a photography business, you may decide to be only an on-location photographer at first, shooting weddings and family portraits on the beach or in local public gardens. If this is the case, then you may not need a brick-and-mortar establishment. If you wish to establish a studio side of the operation to go along with your event shooting, then you will need to make room for the required costs in your plan. It may be prudent to establish phases for your business to help defray the start-up costs, such as starting without a storefront while you establish a clientele, but with plans to open one in six months or a year.

It is important at this stage to evaluate all your costs and options. Keep the notes that you make as you determine the direction you plan to take, since these can be great reference points when it's time to expand your business later.

Something I learned when writing my very first business plan is that there are really two different plans you need to come up with. You need to have an operations plan as well as a plan to raise money. The operations plan will be centered on your specific business model—how you plan to operate and structure your company. The fund-raising presentation should focus more on the industry, the growth projections, the competition, and your position within the marketplace. It should also profile similar companies that have been successful and that have successfully exited. You need to include some of this information in your operations plan, but it is central to your fund-raising plan because it demonstrates an in-depth, working knowledge of the realm you're seeking to enter.

I start with my operational plan and develop that first before moving on to the financial plan. The creation of your operational plan needs to be a bottom-up procedure. Don't start with a number in mind; start from zero and then add expenses and capital requirements, broken down to their most basic components. You should ask yourself, "What do I absolutely have to have to operate this business, and what will that cost me each month?"

To create a hypothetical situation, look at it this way: How many widgets do I need to sell per month in order to cover my expenses? If the answer is one hundred, then determine how many widgets the average salesperson can sell. If the answer is ten, then you know you will need at least ten salespeople—or you need to have marketing that will drive some portion of those sales, say 50 percent, in which case you know you need five people and X dollars in marketing to generate the orders. But for those five or ten employees, you need to figure out their true expense. How much does it cost to recruit them? What will you pay them? How much of their pay will be generated through commissions? Will you be providing them with a cell phone or a laptop? How you will fund their sales calls? But don't just write down a number and move on. You need to consider carefully every miniscule part of the potential cost: Will you pay your employees mileage if they use their own cars? How will you pay for their travel if they need to fly? Will you pay them a per diem? How much money will you provide for each meal? What about lodging?

You have to remember that every single one of those numbers on the page represents a series of decisions and costs that you need to have considered in order to have a firm grasp on the real price of things.

One of the most important things to remember while planning projected costs and budgets is the determination of what your family is going to live on. As we discussed in the preceding chapters, this number should be conservative, but also realistic. You will need to make sure that you factor in the real costs that your family will be facing—not only for your current bills and financial obligations, but also costs you may not currently incur, such as a health insurance policy if you lose coverage when you change jobs. These costs need to be included in your plan, or you will find yourself unable to meet your obligations in the first month, which will put your entire business in jeopardy.

I know it might sound contradictory to mention the importance of a workable income because the previous chapter was all about bracing yourself and your family for dramatic sacrifices, but as I stressed, you should not be reckless. You need to make sure you have enough to survive on and to meet your obligations to the family as a provider. This will allow you to focus your energy on the success of your business and not the potential failure of your family.

In addition, having a realistic amount designated for family finances is an important part of the formula for your investors to see. They want to see a number that is low enough that you will be hungry to work for the next sale but large enough to actually support a family. That shows you have a realistic grasp as to the value and reach of money. It is important to show your investors that you understand a family of four cannot pay a mortgage and all their bills on $15,000 a year. Of course investors want to see that you're ready to sacrifice, but not to the point that it's no longer realistic. That reflects poorly on your grasp of business and marketplace realities.

 **If you're afraid to leave your job because you will lose your health care, you're stuck in employee thinking, which is rooted in the idea that the company has to take care of you. Entrepreneurial thinking is rooted in self-reliance and problem solving.**

And speaking of marketplace realities, I want to give you a strong word of caution about being overly optimistic. Of course you should believe in your company's potential, but it's far too easy to create a million-dollar company on an Excel spreadsheet. On paper, it doesn't seem as farfetched to count on exponential growth—in the first month you grow 20 percent, then 20 percent again in the second month, and in a matter of just a few months, your entire company has doubled in size. Unfortunately, real growth doesn't work that way. You have to write a realistic plan that considers units of transaction backed by marketing support and sales expenses. If I can offer a lesson that I've learned several times, it's not to get overly optimistic in your forecasts. Your investors will turn on you if you miss your numbers. A mentor and former board member of mine, Gordon Watson, once told me, "Ryan, a CEO has never been fired for missing his numbers, only for missing his forecasts." I took his point seriously.

Ten years ago, many investors would be willing to fund wildly ambitious business plans, but those days are past us. Now, you need to prove exactly *how* you will be able to achieve your sales goals; it's not enough to simply state what they are. Spend a lot of time on the top line. What is your revenue going to be? Make sure you have a firm grasp on exactly how that will be achieved. The bottom line will come, but you need to have a firm sense of how the top line will be achieved for your plan to be viable.

As you reach the completion of your business plan and feel you have your numbers solidly in place, it may be worth it to make a small investment in hiring an accountant or a lawyer to look it over and double-check that everything looks right. Obviously, he or she may not be able to speak to the specific circumstances of starting a business in your field, but he or she can ensure that what you've designated for salaries, taxes, insurance, and any other legally required costs are in line with and appropriate to the size of the company you are establishing.

Also, as elementary as it sounds, you will want to carefully proofread every element of your plan more than once. Read it word for word and aloud, if you have to. Correct anything that sounds wordy, awkward, or unclear, and definitely check for typos. It's an unfortunate truth, but given the number of business plans investors get each year, they are all looking for a reason to eliminate each one to quickly pare down their "to consider" stack. Typos can come across as careless, and no one wants to invest in a company whose CEO is not detail oriented. Treat your business plan just as you would your own résumé if you were applying for a job with the investor because, in a way, that's exactly what it is—a résumé for your company. Make sure your first impression is a positive one. If you are going to submit a plan to me, make sure it is concise. If there's one thing that makes me dismiss a plan quickly, it's a plan that is too verbose. These days, a PowerPoint presentation with no more than thirty slides is all you need for your investor presentation.

Finally, there is one last piece of the business plan puzzle that is, perhaps, the key to making everything else work: You have to be entrepreneurial minded, not employee minded.

Too many people are stuck in the mindset of thinking like employees instead of thinking like the boss. If you're afraid to leave your job because you will lose your health care, you're stuck in employee thinking, which is rooted in the idea that the company has to take care of you. Entrepreneurial thinking is rooted in self-reliance and problem solving.

Rather than worry about what benefits you're going to lose, you need to get yourself to a place where your emotional reflexes are honed to finding solutions. Don't think, "I'm stuck here because I can't give up my health care plan." Instead, get yourself in the mindset of thinking, "Does this new venture mean a loss of health insurance? Then I need to find a policy that I can work into my business plan."

You absolutely, positively have to start thinking in a way that is solution oriented if you are going to be the one in charge; there is no passing the buck in your own company. The buck stops with you.

If you haven't already made the transition to this mode of thinking, then you must do so while you are composing your business plan. Otherwise, you're wasting your time. People who think like employees will always be employees. People who think like entrepreneurs will be the ones who climb the ranks to become something more than an expendable employee. You are not just an employee in your company anymore—you are the boss, the lifeline, the backbone.

Welcome to the world of entrepreneurship.

CHAPTER 7

CAPITALIZING YOUR BUSINESS

Money makes the world go 'round.

It sounds a little cynical, but it's the truth. No idea, no matter how good, and no business plan, no matter how tightly written, will ever get off the ground without funding. And if small businesses are the backbone of the economy, and the American economy is the most powerful in the world . . .

In chapter 10 we talk about the three types of businesses—traditional, franchise, and Direct Sales—and we help you determine which business model is best for you. Some entrepreneurs I work with don't want the headache of raising capital, so they choose a route that doesn't require fund raising. If you are one of these types, I completely understand, as it can be all-consuming and counterproductive to your business goals.

If you are planning to launch a traditional business or open a franchise, your next move—securing capital for your business—is the make-or-break point. If you can raise the funds you need to start out, you will have all the chance in the world at success. If you can't, you will never get that shot. I've raised as little as $15,000 from an investor and as much as over $15 million—and I can assure you that no matter the amount, it is *all* hard work.

The most important advice I can offer as we begin this discussion is that no matter the source of the money, you have to be willing to earn it. If you aren't willing, then none of what follows in this chapter or this book will be of any use to you because you are not thinking like an entrepreneur.

No matter who you turn to—be it family, friends, banks, or investors—no one should offer you a dime if you are not able to assure them that you will go to your grave trying to earn a return for their money. And if you don't make that promise, probably no one *will* invest, either. Keep that in mind as we outline the process, because that will necessarily color everything else that goes into securing investments.

Often, the biggest challenge is knowing where to start. It's no secret that many sources for capital have dried up, with banks going under, banks tightening up lending practices, and many investors losing huge amounts of money in the stock market.

 **Do not let the terms of your financial agreement become the focus of your relationship. Do not over-discuss business at family gatherings unless people ask you about it. Do not pressure your friends to invest if they are not completely comfortable with the idea. And don't ask for investments beyond what you know they can afford.**

What do you do when you don't have a business—just a business plan—and you're selling an idea rather than a product? How do you start securing those first few investments that give you the momentum to keep going and chase the next possible investor?

For many people, that starting point is family and friends. This makes sense, of course—they know you, they know your work ethic, and they are probably already familiar with your business plan to some degree.

But you need to be careful. Money issues have strained or ruined countless relationships. If you turn to your relatives or close friends for financing, you will need to make sure that the effort you put into making their investment grow is greater than even they could have hoped for. Remember that if you fail to get them their return, it may cost more than just the dollar amount. It could cost the friendship. Just because someone knows your work ethic doesn't mean that you can skip over that part of your presentation. Treat interested family and friends as you would any other potential investor. You will probably talk to them differently, of course, but make sure they have the same ironclad promise of your commitment to this project that you would give to a business-person or a loan officer at a bank.

Tell them the truth: Whenever a company is starting up, there are going to be challenges. There are always going to be rocky patches, even for the most seasoned entrepreneurs. Personally, I've had people tell me countless times that my venture was going to fail. Over time, my response to the naysayers has been simple: "If it does fail, I'll be ashamed, but I'll never know it." This always gets a few quizzical looks until someone asks me what I mean.

"Simply this," I tell them. "I'll never know about the failure because you will be talking about it at my funeral—I'm going to succeed, or I'll be dead trying. I will never accept that it's going to fail. The company might mutate, it might evolve, it might change, I might change—everything might change—but it is not going to fail. I'm going to be successful at this venture one way or the other."

Give this same kind of assurance to your relatives. Be sure that your friends have such a level of confidence in you that when they write that check, they know that it is going to be put to the best possible use.

This can be a very tenuous issue, so proceed with caution. Do not let the terms of your financial agreement become the focus of your relationship. Do not over-discuss business at family gatherings unless people ask you about it. Do not pressure your friends to invest if they are not completely comfortable with the idea. And don't ask for investments beyond what you know they can afford.

Of course you want your family and friends to support you and to share in your success when the business becomes profitable. But do not risk putting a strain on those relationships by making the other person feel pressured to invest if he or she is not interested or not comfortable with venture capital. Remember what we stressed before: Entrepreneurship is not for everyone. Some people are simply not risk takers. Do not harm your friendship or family ties by trying to change them, and do not be hurt if they choose not to invest. You are going to need emotional support from the people closest to you as you launch your business, and you do not want to alienate the very people who can provide that for you.

For those who do appreciate what you're doing, though, and believe in your business plan, make sure that you pay them back promptly—and first. In other words, you get paid last. Your investors get paid first. Always. From the largest investor to the smallest, they get first dibs at the profits, and you get what is left. After all, you are being paid by the business to manage it; when there is a profit, your investors should reap the benefits, too. In addition to making sure you work to earn each investment, that is the most hard-and-fast rule I can offer.

Probably the number-one reason why I am where I am today is because I paid back everybody who gave me money for my businesses. People can look at me and say, "For every dollar I gave him, he gave me five back," or, "I gave him $100,000 in 2003, and he gave me $200,000 in 2004." Big or small, it doesn't matter. You have to look out for your investors first because without them, you have no business and no profits. The return you yield for your investors will pay you dividends forever.

That's how you keep and build relationships when you're asking for money from family, friends, or anyone else. You make sure that they get paid back, even if you yourself have nothing to show for it at first. When people see their money come back to them having accomplished something and grown, they see that you are trustworthy and reliable enough to invest in again. Often, it can finally help convince more reluctant investors to join as well. It's like your mother always told you when you were small: You build relationships by putting others first. You ruin them by looking out only for yourself. Never forget that.

While there are a number of different ways to raise money—debt, common stock, preferred stock—when starting a new business, I usually recommend convertible debt to get started. The way this method works is that you provide your investors with a note stipulating that their investment amount can either be repaid with interest and a premium within a set amount of time (usually a year) or converted to equity in the company at a discount to the then-present value of the company, at the discretion of the investor or the company, or at mutual discretion. This instrument can be constructed inexpensively, and it provides flexibility to both parties. I have used this method several times and have also invested in start-ups that initially offered convertible debt.

If your business proves successful, most investors will opt for a share of equity so they can continue to gain returns on their investment. However, the option of repaying the loan in full is an important option to keep on the table if you either want to retain complete and total ownership of the company or, perhaps even more important, if you find that an investor has proven difficult to work with. From personal experience, I have found that repaying the loan, the interest, and the premium was worth every cent to end the relationship with certain investors who were unpleasant, unreasonable, or otherwise undesirable partners.

Recently, I made an angel investment of $100,000 in a new company where the terms of my loan were either 20 percent interest repaid within one year or an investment conversion to 30 percent equity in the company. Now, I have to admit that I wouldn't mind holding such a large stake because the company seems to be a very promising one. However, for the sake of the entrepreneurs starting up the business, I hope that they are able to repay me and retain ownership of their work.

If this is your approach, you need to be generous, but not unreasonable, with your interest and equity rate offerings. The newer your company, the more generous you will have to be because you won't have as much leverage. The deal I mentioned above is highly favorable for me, but I was also their first investor and they were willing to take a bigger risk to secure the large amount of capital they needed to launch their plan.

Common stock and preferred stock get much trickier. Common stock functions just like stock in a publicly owned company does. The gains from it are tied to the company's market value and performance.

Preferred stock is a very complicated instrument. A preferred stock subscription agreement can cost tens of thousands of dollars to create and, if not done correctly, can cost you your company. If an investor will only invest in preferred stock, you should hire a great attorney. This lesson was one of my most expensive early on in my career. I didn't know enough about the rights I had agreed to in my preferred stock agreement. And when the company eventually sold, it cost me millions.

The challenge that preferred stocks present is that unless you have a very firm grasp on how the system works, you can find yourself in a position to lose everything when it's time to sell your company. This actually happened to me at one sale when everyone was gathered and the lawyer began handing out spreadsheets with the payout amount earned by each member written inside. We were going to sign the papers that afternoon to complete the sale, and we were all in an elated mood—and then I looked at my number and saw the number "0" looking back at me. Here was a company I had labored on with my own blood, sweat, and tears, and because I had not thoroughly understood the terms of the preferred equity rights, I was going to be left with absolutely nothing upon its sale.

Thankfully for me, the other board members quickly agreed that this arrangement was unacceptable, and we were able to negotiate a different deal that would allow me a share of the proceeds. But that experience taught me the importance of understanding something completely or not signing my name to the contract. Now, with a number of years and several more businesses under my belt, I feel confident enough to work with stock as a form of fund-raising. In fact, when we were getting ready to start ViSalus, we first raised about $200,000 in debt and then $1.5 million in preferred stock. We were then able to use some of the proceeds from the preferred stock to pay off the debt. Of course, it took a lot more fundraising later to get the company where it is today. This was only an approach we took because time and hard experience had helped me to understand how to structure the transaction to meet the needs of all parties.

But how do you land that first big deal? How to you capture the attention of someone who can offer you a substantial sum that can launch your business to the next level? Banks and investors are continually getting applications and proposals for loans. As we discussed in the last chapter, you have to be able to make yourself and your business plan stand out by offering something unique, superior, or edgy—this is called having points of differentiation.

When it comes to raising capital, though, there is one more aspect that really trumps them all: you have to offer value. I'm not talking about profit potential here, though obviously that is part of the equation. What really makes the first impression, what helps you to get your foot in the door, is that you demonstrate to the investors the lengths to which you will go to get them a valuable return on their money. And for most people who are in the position to invest, time is their most limited—and, therefore, most valuable—resource.

 **One of the most effective ways to assure investors that you are willing to earn their capital is to offer them equity in your company. This not only shows the investors that you're willing to sacrifice for your company, but it also gives them even more motivation to assist you in making the company profitable because it directly impacts their own returns.**

You have to show your potential investors the effort you are willing to make to accommodate their schedule and meet their needs. This not only creates a strong first impression, but it also demonstrates that you are a go-getter who will exert yourself to do what it takes to make your business succeed.

I learned this lesson early on, when I took a gamble and asked to arrange a meeting with one of the founders of Sun Microsystems. I made a five-hour drive from Los Angeles to San Louis Obispo for a very short meeting with him because I wanted his advice. I didn't even pitch to him at that first meeting. I just asked for his advice in launching, growing, and sustaining my new start-up business. But later, I knew I could pick up the phone or send him an e-mail to ask, "Could you take a look at this business plan?" because I had first demonstrated to him that I understood how valuable his time was, both to him as well as to me.

Putting forth effort like that is your first step to demonstrating that you are willing to earn any investment someone might decide to offer you. The advantage of securing one or two larger investors through efforts like this is that those investors can often open the doors to a number of other investors. After all, the goal of any investment is to make a profit, and any investor is going to want your business to grow and succeed. The more investors who are able to offer up capital, the more rapidly the business can expand its offerings and thus, by extension, its client base, which leads to increased sales and profits.

Therefore, by securing a few "anchor investors" early on, your business will not only have credibility with other venture capitalists, but networking opportunities are also likely to expand exponentially.

But how can you assure those anchor investors that you are willing to earn their capital? One of the most effective ways is to offer them equity in your company in exchange for their time. This not only shows the investors that you're willing to sacrifice for your company, but it also gives them even more motivation to assist you in making the company profitable because it directly impacts their own returns.

When SkyPipeline was still in its early days, Fred Warren agreed to help me raise $1 million to expand it. At the time, my company was doing about $30,000 in sales per month, but we negotiated a deal where he would contribute about one-half of the $1 million I needed, and in the meantime, he would introduce me to a number of other potential investors. Not only did my business grow, but I benefited from fantastic mentorship from someone who had been in business for years and wanted to make sure that his money, as well as the money of his friends, was being put to good use. It was an invaluable lesson, not just from a monetary point of view, but also because of what I was able to learn from Fred's interest in my business and in my business skills.

Fred taught me how to be a CEO, but just as important, he introduced me to the Goergen family, who were and still are some of my most valuable contacts. Your reputation with investors is something you will carry with you throughout your career, so guard it well.

Now, chances are that you will not need nearly as substantial a sum to start your business as I required. But if you are able to make a few key connections and establish credibility with local business leaders or venture capitalists in your area, you may be able to open doors to larger investments as well as smaller ones.

However, I need to offer two warnings to keep in the forefront of your mind when the large investments and/or profits start to roll in. Venture capital relationships are arrangements that are successful only if you are very knowledgeable in how to structure the transaction, if you are smart in choosing with whom you work, and if you are able to keep it all in focus. Surround yourself with the right people who have the right values, philosophies, and intentions with their investments. Whenever money is involved, there is a definite sense of obligation, and you do not want to find yourself in any partnerships with anyone of questionable character, which may not only cause problems in terms of your own alliances and commitments, but it also can hurt your reputation with other, more credible investors.

Additionally, you have to make sure that you keep yourself grounded in terms of how you think about money. It's very tempting, once the profits start rolling in, to think that your days of sacrificing are over. When I sold SkyPipeline as part of a merger, it ended up being a $25 million deal. The newspapers wrote about how I had made so much money as a young kid in my twenties. I had every Wall Street banker calling me. My mom and my hometown crowd were all so proud. I thought I had arrived. But I didn't get $25 million in cash. I had been heavily diluted for additional financing rounds, and the actual amount of cash, although significant, would not allow me to retire happily on an island somewhere.

So even though it looked as though I had made a massive windfall, it was a much smaller number than everyone thought—but I kept the story going. I loved that people thought I was a wildly successful multimillionaire, and I started spending as if I were, until I finally got myself in check. You always have to be mindful of what was discussed in chapter 5. You have to keep yourself in a save-and-invest rather than spend-what-I've-got-and-more mentality.

You are your company's biggest investor. Other people may put in more money, but you give money, time, and a piece of yourself for the business. Because of that, you have to be smart about your personal investments, no matter where you are in the game. You have to use your profits to grow the business rather than to just let it coast, or you'll find your investors and your customers looking elsewhere and dropping off one by one. You have to stay hungry for the next sale or you won't be able to attract any more interested investors, because your commitment to the company's success won't be as apparent.

Part of maintaining that drive is to try to project confidence at all times, no matter what. That doesn't mean that you manipulate the numbers to look better than they are—that's unethical, on top of being bad business. It's impossible to make definite promises about returns because you never know what the future will hold, but you should always leave your investors with the sense that if you say you're going to achieve a certain goal, then they have no reason to doubt that you really will.

The best example of this that I can offer from my own life occurred as I was trying to grow the nutraceutical company, ViSalus. Nick Sarnicola and Blake Mallen had already begun marketing the line of physician-designed vitamins and supplements when they approached me for an investment pitch. My weight was out of control, and my health was not where it needed to be for my age. So I was interested in what they had to say and impressed by the rock-solid patents they had for the products.

 **Confidence is the key. You should never be dishonest or misrepresent yourself or your company, but you need to be willing to go out on a limb, set goals, and let your investors see the level of belief you have in your product as well as your ability to sell it.**

I decided to invest, and I became a major shareholder in the company. I knew we had the potential to expand, so I began to reach out to potential investors, including Todd Goergen. I had made Todd five times his initial investment in SkyPipeline, so I knew he thought highly of me as an entrepreneur. But I also knew that I was going to have to earn my future investments with him, too. I thought it was worth a shot to give him a call to see whether I might be able to make something of that connection.

I called him up and said, "I'm going to be in New York next week, and I'd like to come see you and talk about this deal." Now, the only reason I was planning to go to New York was to meet with him, but he didn't need to know that. I casually asked to meet with him, and as far as he was concerned, I was there on business—because I was. That business just happened to concern him.

He looked at his calendar and said, "All right, I'll be in Wednesday. Are you going to be around? If so, meet me at the Racquet Club." Wednesday came, and there I was at one of the most famous hangouts of the New York power elite, sipping tea and talking business. I gave my sales pitch, he looked at our numbers, and then he shook his head. "It looks good, but it's too small for me. It's not big enough to pique my interest."

I asked him how big we would need to be to entice him. He answered, "About $200,000 a month." At that point, the company was clearing about $40,000 a month, which meant we would have to more than quadruple the size of the company before we could hope to have Todd on board.

But instead of just counting the meeting as a loss, I thought about the confidence that Nick and Blake had exhibited that had won me over, and I took the same route. Smiling, I drank the last of my tea and said, "Well then, I'll be calling you back very soon."

When I got back to California, I met with my business partners and told them, "I think we've got an investor—he just doesn't know it yet. We're going to get to $200,000 and then we will call him and say, 'We did what you told us to do. What's our next goal?'" That's exactly what we did, and it paid off. While we were building toward our new goal, I was also rallying friends and other interested parties who were willing to invest almost an equal amount in capital for future growth.

In December of that same year, Todd agreed to invest and came on as a partner in parity with Nick, Blake, and me. It had taken a lot of guts and a lot of work, but we'd gotten our investors, and they set their sights on helping us build our business to a $100 million plus company.

Confidence is the key. You should never be dishonest or misrepresent yourself or your company, but you need to be willing to go out on a limb, set goals, and let your investors see the level of belief you have in your product as well as your ability to sell it.

Do not confuse confidence with bravado or self-importance, though. No one wants to be a business partner with someone who is cocky or acts as if he or she is superior. That's not confidence—that's just obnoxious.

Quite often, I find myself faced with entrepreneurs who treat my invitation to make their sales pitch as a ploy to steal from them. I've had owners of brand new businesses that have not even launched insist that I sign a nondisclosure agreement before they will agree to speak with me. I don't even know who they are or what their product does, and they are asking me to sign a legal document? That does not make a good first impression on any potential investor.

If I balk at signing anything before I at least meet with them, the response I usually get from these entrepreneurs is basically one that accuses me of premeditated theft, as if I were only interested in meeting with them to take their ideas and market them myself. If the new product has a patent, as many of them do, the investor will often act as if this is a trump card that gives him or her total legitimacy and commands my respect. In this kind of situation, the request for capital is usually a rather high amount—and again, all for a product that I don't know anything about.

It happens with e-mails, too. I get dozens of letters from people who basically say, "I have the best idea in the world, and I need you to fund it, but I can't tell you what it is because you might steal it." Not only is that insulting to me person-ally, but it also demonstrates to me that the person does not have a grasp on the interpersonal skills needed to raise money, let alone to interact with customers. If he or she has not taken the time to figure out what my motivations, needs, and business practices are, how is this person going to treat a client? I always have to fight the urge to e-mail back, "If your product is so great that I should invest in it sight unseen, then you don't need me because it should be selling itself."

Be sure to avoid that kind of self-important approach to raising capital. Confidence is essential, but it should be humble confidence. Of course you want to protect yourself and your ingenuity, but be careful to avoid letting your hard work make you cocky. Don't act as if you are doing the investors a favor by giving your pitch; remember, you want to be offering something to them—something of value. Thank them for their time, and then outline your plans and goals as well as what their place is in all of them.

Too many entrepreneurs fall into the trap of thinking that confidence means acting as if you don't need any help from anyone. That's ridiculous. Obviously, if you didn't need help, you wouldn't be out making the presentation and asking for funding. Confidence is endearing; overconfidence is alienating.

I want to include a quick list of dos and don'ts for pitching to an investor— because as obvious as some of these items may seem, they all address very common mistakes or missteps that can cost you the deal:

- Do turn off your cell phone before the presentation, and do not wear an earpiece.

- Do dress professionally—that means a business suit or a shirt and tie. Casual wear is never appropriate in this kind of setting. There is nothing casual about success.

- Do be sure to ask for the investment at the end of your presentation.

- Do rehearse your presentation a minimum of three times.

- Don't allow your presentation to run over thirty minutes, and be sure to allow at least fifteen extra minutes for a question-and-answer session at the end.

- Do end the talk by reciting the specific *actions* that were requested.

- Do follow up on everything to which you committed.

- Don't interrupt your prospective investor when he or she is talking.

- Do make sure to answer the investor's question clearly and concisely, and ask him or her after you speak, "Did that answer your question?"

- Don't answer questions if you don't know the answer. Say, "I don't know, but I will follow up with you on that question."

- Do make sure your investment presentation is printed in color and bound professionally.

- Don't ever respond with negative emotion to a criticism or lack of interest from a potential investor.

It's a tough world out there, requiring a delicate balance of persuasiveness but not pressure, extreme sacrifice but not self-destruction, and great confidence and genuine humility. Raising capital is probably going to be the most difficult part of establishing your business. You must be willing to work yourself to the very brink to secure each investment and then continue to work yourself to the brink to make sure you get a return. It's definitely not easy—if it were, everyone would be doing it.

If you determine that you are, in fact, one of the few people with the right combination of strength, determination, levelheadedness, and tenacity to take the challenge, then I congratulate you because the risk is great, but the rewards are even greater.

Should you decide to follow this advice, you're going to discover a lot about yourself, you're going to build your business plan even further, you're going to be thinking about your financial model in ways that you probably weren't, and you're going to produce something greater than what you had when you started. I can't guarantee you're going to raise money, but I can guarantee that you are going to get closer than you would have otherwise.

Author's Note: I'm interested in working with America's best and brightest aspiring entrepreneurs. Please contact me through nothingtolose.com and, who knows, I might become an investor in your business.

CHAPTER 8

LOOK FOR STANDARDS AND LEARN

We all have heroes. Who didn't spend hours in the yard as a kid pretending that he was Michael Jordan or Derek Jeter? Or in front of a mirror with an imaginary microphone pretending that she was Madonna? It's just human nature to want to imitate those whom we admire—and that shouldn't stop just because we're now in the business world.

There is a reason that we admire the people we do. They espouse something that strikes a chord within us. Be it their innate talent, drive, wisdom, or attitude, there is a reason we find certain individuals fascinating, and if we can harness that same spark that made them great, perhaps we can achieve greatness as well.

Evaluate the purpose statement you composed while working on your business plan. What are the philosophies and goals that you outlined in it? What business leaders espouse those values in their own corporations, careers, and personal lives? What about other figures outside the corporate world whose lives have affected your beliefs and perspectives? It is here that you should begin to look for the standards and the business models that you hope to emulate within your own company? Who do you want to be as a business leader? Seek out and pursue those standards of excellence.

Consider first those individuals within your industry whose business practices helped define—or redefine—the field.

 **Look for standards and learn who is best at what you want to do. What can you learn from them? Do you copy them? What mistakes have they made that you can avoid?**

If you are in interior design, for example, whose styles have influenced and inspired you? Was it Pierre François Léonard Fontaine, Dorothy Draper, Sister Parish, or Nina Petronzio? Each distinct style made an impact on the industry. Spend a little time researching the pioneers in your field, and discover what it was they did that made their work so memorable.

Or perhaps you are looking to open a clothing boutique. Whose artistry has had the greatest impact on fashion in the last one hundred years? Which lines do you admire, both in decades past and in the present? By reading up on the trendsetters and icons, you can learn what philosophies and practices shaped the industry.

In other words, ask yourself who the groundbreakers are in your field. Study what they did that was so revolutionary, whether it was something dramatically new or a revitalization of something old. This can help you define your own unique approach to the market. Look for standards and learn who is best at what you want to do. What can you learn from them? Do you copy them? What mistakes have they made that you can avoid?

At the same time, however, our heroes are not always headline-grabbing figures. Sometimes we are drawn to people whose contributions are quiet but still memorable in their own way. Perhaps there is a photographer whose work was never as famous as that of Ansel Adams or Dorothea Lange, but whose photographs have a quality about them that make them distinct. You always know when you spot them in a *Time Life* collection or a *National Geographic* magazine. Study those people and the philosophies behind their work. Learn everything you can about what made them successful, both in terms of how they practiced their craft and in how they handled their business affairs.

In my early twenties, I stumbled across a tape of one of Tony Robbins's speeches, and I was mesmerized. He was so dynamic and engaging that I hung on his every word, wanting not only to understand everything he was saying, but also to learn how he was doing it—what made him so convincing, so trustworthy, so likable. I read everything about him that I could, and the more I learned, the more I respected the way he encouraged people to take responsibility for their own lives and to take action to better their circumstances.

I knew that someday, that was what I wanted to do. I wanted to empower people. I wanted to speak to crowds to make them feel optimistic and motivated. Tony Robbins represented everything that I wanted to do, and he did it better than anyone else I knew.

That's why it is so important to pursue something you love—chances are good that it's an interest or a talent that has been following you for years. Think back to the figures you were drawn to as a child. Do any of them still inspire you? How many of those heroes are tied to the business you are now planning to open, be it a dance school or a bakery? Did you love Mikhail Baryshnikov or Julia Child? Study them now, from an adult point of view, and see what you can learn about what made them so great. Return to those figures who first inspired you, and allow them to inspire you all over again.

But don't just limit your scope to those professionals you'd like to emulate; you can learn a tremendous amount by studying the habits and philosophies of companies and leaders you *don't* want to be like, too.

This is something I do regularly. Especially in the field of computer science and technology, which is where most of my interest lies, I look at companies I want to be like and those I don't. I read everything I can to learn about their business models and what is working for them and how I can hold my own company to that standard—and everything that is not working in companies whose stock is falling or whose corner in the market is crumbling. Every time a person leaves a company like Google and writes a book, I am the first person in line to buy it. In chapter 12, we will discuss the importance of being a student of your industry, but right now, I want you to delve into the study of business leadership to discover as much as you can about how to structure and operate your business according to the standards you admire and hope to achieve through your work.

And to do so, you don't have to stay focused only on your own industry. It is a good starting place, but I would urge you to research leaders who may be outside your field but whose vision has proved successful through solid business practices and innovative solutions. It could be a Fortune 500 CEO, or it could be your entrepreneurial uncle—the point is that you need to seek out people you admire and learn from them.

Do you want your business to stay a locally based one, whose management is kept within the family and whose product or service meets area-specific needs? Or do you have dreams of one day expanding your company into a national or international, industry-leading powerhouse?

If you desire the first, then you should try to interview people in your area who have done just that—perhaps a carpentry business or local trucking company that has become a fixture in the community through several generations. Find out what unique challenges your area presents and what each business found was the key to its longevity. Learn what practices and philosophies have kept it firmly rooted in your town and what each company president feels is the secret to gaining credibility and maintaining customer loyalty among locals and newcomers alike.

Reach out to those people you already know and respect who represent that ideal. If you are starting a landscaping business, your uncle with a plumbing service might not seem as if he has much to offer you in terms of advice, but he is probably a treasure trove of wisdom about how to hire the right people, deal with difficult customers, and stay visible within the community. Resources like these are invaluable as you seek to establish the standards by which you plan to operate.

On the other hand, if you have large-scale aspirations, look to companies like Walmart, Walgreens, or Barnes & Noble, which all started as small, local retailers but grew to become massive, multibillion-dollar corporations.

But don't just look at what they represent in terms of size; study the business model. Walmart is the quintessential big-box store, with generalized merchandise and groceries for one-stop, comprehensive shopping. Walgreens, on the other hand, is much more specialized in its stock—it is primarily a pharmacy and drug store with a few grocery items included for convenience. Barnes & Noble is a highly specialized chain that focuses on books, magazines, and related items. Each company is a standout success story in its field, but they operate under different models.

Even though you may not be interested in opening a grocery store, pharmacy, or bookshop, if you are looking at retail, you may want to study what each of these companies has done to grow beyond its original business plan. Barnes & Noble, for example, became the first bookstore to advertise on television when the company aired its first commercial in 1974. By embracing the media and venturing into a type of advertising otherwise unexplored in the field of booksellers, Barnes & Noble began a climb to the top of its industry. Nowadays, it is going to take something far more innovative than a television commercial to be groundbreaking with your business, but by investigating business models you admire, you can gain a deeper understanding of what works and why— and you can make those same goals part of your company's standards.

Consider, too, the business leaders with whom you most closely identify. For example, if you are an entrepreneurial young woman, you might find yourself drawn to someone like Ivanka Trump, who epitomizes a savvy business persona with a uniquely female perspective. If you are older, you might find yourself more interested in her father, Donald, who had an empire, lost it, and rebuilt it through tenacity and toughness. If you are African-American, you might find yourself especially drawn to prominent African-American business leaders like Richard Nanula, who became the CFO of Disney at age thirty-one.

The point is that we live in an era of incredible diversity; anywhere you look, you can find inspiration from people who represent part of who you are or who share a part of your personal identity. Whether it is age, gender, race, faith, or ability/disability—whatever is important to you will be important to your business. If a commonality helps connect you to an individual's story or circumstances, take a closer look at what he or she has to say along those lines. That person can often offer valuable pointers for someone like you who shares an aspect of the individual's identity.

Now is also the time to begin really reaching out to the mentors you identified back when you were defining your assets. Learn everything you can about their business practices so you can enact some of those standards into your own company's operations. You should be willing not only to identify those standards you wish to emulate, but also to learn how to put them into practice.

Whether it's a smaller or larger business that has piqued your interest, seek out meetings with the men and women who head it up. I've always just believed that if I exerted myself to demonstrate my respect for the value of their time, and if they were willing to spend a few minutes to teach me as someone who is aspiring to be where they are, then it was a winning proposition all around. I get to learn from their experience, and they are reminded of how far they've come. I have never been afraid to network with people—not even the famous or powerful elite. I have been nervous about it, but never afraid. You have to be willing to at least write a letter, make a phone call, or reach out in some way to ask for that meeting. If you don't at least try, you'll never even have the chance.

Before you go into a meeting with a mentor, you should make sure that you prepare thoroughly. Remember, time is a valuable resource to executives, so make sure you make the most of it. Ask insightful and thoughtful questions that will open you up to valuable—and maybe even unexpected—answers. Know what questions to avoid, such as sensitive topics that are likely to irritate them. You aren't a journalist trying to get to the bottom of a story, you're an entrepreneur trying to absorb the best lessons you can.

Lawyers have an old saying: "Don't ask any question you don't already know the answer to." When it comes to meeting with mentors, that is the worst advice you could possibly follow. Don't waste your time or theirs with questions that can be learned through research.

Here's another proverb: Never ask a question you can find out otherwise. Find out company statistics and the basics of the person's life through the various Internet resources available. Do your homework; do the legwork. This will help you get right to the point when you finally get the opportunity to interview that person face-to-face.

I recently received a great interview tip from the former Louisiana State University basketball coach Dale Brown. When he was offered his first head coach position in 1972, he made a list of people he wanted to interview who had the standards of speaking, public relations, and coaching that he hoped to incorporate into his own program. At the top of his list was legendary UCLA basketball coach John Wooden.

But when Dale sat down to come up with a list of questions to ask this icon of his sport, he froze up and was completely at a loss as to where he should even start. Finally, he pulled out a notebook and wrote down the alphabet, using each letter to prompt ideas for his questions. When he went out to visit Coach Wooden, he ended up staying for five days and filling several notebooks full of ideas, tips, advice, and wisdom on a wide variety of issues, thanks to his alphabet notes.

Most of us will not be privileged enough to get five whole days with our mentors, but this is a great story to show the importance of preparation before such a meeting.

Make the most of every mentoring opportunity you get. Take the time to prepare yourself to get the most out of any meeting with a more-experienced businessperson. It could be an ongoing, long-term mentorship arrangement like the one I had with Todd Goergen, or it could just be a half-hour meeting with someone whose words will stay with you as you make operational decisions. Either way, make sure that you seize the chance put into practice the years of experience that person has been willing to share with you.

These opportunities are an important part of developing into a better and more effective business leader. If you find someone who is willing to mentor you in an ongoing relationship, you should definitely jump on that offer. Never let him or her seize control of your management, but definitely listen when your mentor raises concerns and advises you to take certain actions.

Fred Warren was just such a mentor for me. When he first took an interest in SkyPipeline, he saw a company with a lot of potential being run by a kid who had very little experience. He recognized that with a little training—sometimes in the form of encouragement and sometimes in the form of tough love—that I had the potential to be a very successful businessman.

The lessons he offered me were tremendous. He introduced me to leaders of several successful companies so I could see how they managed their businesses, how they leveraged deals, and how they interacted with colleagues and customers. Occasionally he would call my attention to a situation that he felt needed to be addressed but that I might not have had enough experience to recognize or to know how to handle appropriately.

I remember that he once advised me to let go of my sales manager. I was shocked—I didn't want to fire anyone. But Fred explained, "Ryan, your sales are terrible right now. You're not meeting goals, and you're not recruiting the number of customers you need to sustain the level of growth that you've been working toward." He showed me that I needed to put what was best for the business ahead of what might make me feel uncomfortable. If someone were not carrying his weight, he needed to be let go. Otherwise, I was not keeping my promise to my investors.

The lessons were tough ones to learn sometimes. But because of the wisdom he was able to offer, thanks to decades of experience, I was able to avoid a lot of rookie mistakes that might have cost me far more time and money than I could afford. Sometimes I was thickheaded, sometimes I would argue with him, and sometimes I would fight with him. But looking back, I realized that he was usually right; now I give Fred a lot of credit for teaching me how to be a CEO.

Finally, you should look for your standards from those people who are not necessarily in your field or even in business at all, but who are simply people whose lives and integrity you admire. Seek out those people, whether through books or articles or even in person.

Whom do you admire? Warren Buffet? John Wooden? Tony Dungy? Teddy Roosevelt? Your grandmother, who lived more devotedly to the "waste not, want not" principle than anyone else you've ever known? It doesn't matter who the person is, so long as you can learn from the model that he or she offers of leadership, thriftiness, motivation—or anything else that you believe is worth emulating. Look for people who will add value to your life.

If you can't arrange a face-to-face meeting, read every book and article you can find, by or about that person. Interview family members and friends, if your hero has passed; learn stories about him or her you may have never heard. All of these efforts will give dimension, depth, and perspective to the rules by which you intend to operate your business.

I have at least thirty people I can name who have given me specific, life-changing wisdom and advice that I have used to become a better person. Some of my

 **You should be open and willing to use every one of the lessons that these figures offer to create a stronger identity within yourself of your beliefs and goals. You will need to have a firm sense of who *you* are and the standards by which you live your life before you can impart those standards onto your business with any real effectiveness.**

mentors spent more time with me than others. Some I learned from only once, but they will have forever contributed to my life: my mother, my stepfather, my very first technology and entrepreneurial mentor, my first venture capitalist mentors, and even my father. The lessons these people have taught me in what to do, how to think, and what to value—as well as what mistakes to avoid—have shaped me into the person I am. There have been countless others who have changed my life and are still changing my life today: Benjamin Franklin, Abraham Lincoln, Martin Luther King Jr., John F. Kennedy—the list goes on.

The point is that you should be open and willing to use every one of the lessons that these figures offer to create a stronger identity within yourself of your beliefs and goals. You will need to have a firm sense of who *you* are and the standards by which you live your life before you can impart those standards onto your business with any real effectiveness.

This isn't a feel-good speech; this is a serious charge. If you want to succeed, you must have a clear definition of what you will and will not do to gain customers, make sales, and achieve your goals. Without those standards in place and ingrained into your life, your business will suffer from an identity crisis, and your employees and clients alike will sense a disconnect between the company's ideals and real life.

Not having standards isn't an option, and they aren't something you can only half-heartedly adhere to. Achievement goals, effective managerial styles, and solid business ethics are a real and vital part of making your company succeed and creating a product that your customers and investors can trust.

Examine your business plan closely, and make sure that your strategy for success is in line with the standards you want to embrace. Then pursue those standards—and the people who embody them—with everything you have.

I used to be really impressed by the typical status symbols in our culture. I was absolutely impressed if someone had a Ferrari parked out front, was sporting a Rolex, or had an Andy Warhol painting hanging in her foyer. That meant they had made it—that meant they were truly successful, right? That was what I wanted.

Thankfully, I've grown past gaping at shallow attempts to flash wealth. You can tell a lot about a person by what his or her prized possession is. For me, the items I now seek to collect are not anything that would fetch a fortune at Sotheby's, but instead they are treasures that represent the wisdom, strength, and integrity I've been privileged enough to encounter in my life. Rather than something intended to impress someone else, I want something that reminds me of how to be a better businessman, employer, philanthropist, and person.

I have first-edition, signed copies of the two books that meant the most to me when I was first starting out: *Think and Grow Rich*, by Napoleon Hill, and *How to Win Friends and Influence People*, by Dale Carnegie. I have a framed copy of John Wooden's pyramid of success. I have a photo with Dale Brown. I have a card on my desk from my mother, telling me how proud she is of me.

These are the things with which I want to surround myself. These are the things by which I want people to see and judge me. How well am I living up to the lessons I've learned from each person? These are the things I value, and these are the standards by which I live and conduct my businesses.

I urge you to do the same.

Ryan with legendary coach Dale Brown.

CHAPTER 9

ESTABLISH YOUR GOLDEN RULES

You don't have to be brilliant to be successful. I'm living proof of that.

You need to have solid philosophies and some kind of spirituality or enlightenment that will give you the foundation upon which you can build everything else, such as work ethic, integrity, and character. You also have to have rules by which operate your business—the Golden Rules, I like to call them.

These are the principles that affect the way you think and the way you act and react. These aren't necessarily moral rules, though those are certainly important. The basic principles of business ethics are generally the same across the board. They don't vary much from business to business (though whether everyone operates by those universal standards of ethics is, unfortunately, another issue entirely). Your Golden Rules of business are a little different. They should be the ideas that shape your philosophies for management, making sales, and networking, and for how you regard failure—and these are going to vary from person to person.

For example, I am absolutely terrible at the game Connect Four. I mean, it's embarrassing because I just can't ever seem to win it. You know the deal—you and your opponent take turns going back and forth, dropping red and black disks into the vertical grid with the objective of trying to stack your pieces in some way to get four in a row. It sounds simple enough, right? Not for me.

After losing probably my hundredth game in a row, I finally figured out why I am so bad at it: Connect Four is a game of long-term strategy. You need to be thinking five or six moves out. I am the kind of person who focuses entirely and single-mindedly on the immediate problem at hand. That's how I think and calculate. That's how I solve problems—I pour everything I have into the most pressing issue, and then I move on to the next one so I don't lose focus trying to deal with them all at once.

 **Gain an awareness of your personal management style and philosophies, and assemble a list of rules that play to those strengths and beliefs.**

To a master chess player (or a master Connect Four player, if there is such a thing), that kind of thinking would make me an absolute failure. I am too intent on my next move to anticipate my opponent's move four turns down the road.

But in terms of managing a business, that approach actually works well for me. My strategy for building is that I take all of the details and data and all the overwhelming tasks I have to complete, and I get down to the one thing I have to do first to have the most impact. That's my priority. I will go after that until that is solved, until my management team hates talking about it, until they either give in and fix it themselves or give up and let me fix it. I will point out that the one thing stopping us is a particular issue and insist that we are not going to leave the room until we resolve it.

Now I have managers and executives that we've hired who are brilliant at moves number two through six, and I'm pretty skilled at move number one, which makes for a good team. If you are a five-actions-out mover, find a person who is going to take the next tactical step necessary. If you are out there five moves ahead of the rest of the world, great. That's a skill, a talent, a gift. You're going to be great at Connect Four, and probably business, too, but you're likely to get easily bored with day-to-day tasks. You just need to recognize that keeping an eye out for problems down the road is going to be one of your Golden Rules.

That's what I mean about finding your Golden Rules—gain an awareness of your personal management style and philosophies, and assemble a list of rules that play to those strengths and beliefs.

I'd like to share some of my other rules, so you can see that they are not really anything earth-shaking but just a collection of quotes, concisely phrased ideas, and general reminders that I keep close to me as I make decisions for my company. I've just picked them up over the years, reading them in magazines or trade journals or hearing them from other people, and one or two I've come up with on my own, and I just like how they capture the point.

I've divided them into five categories, depending on which area of my business they speak to: Communication and Management Rules, Business Model Rules, Customer Rules, Strategy Rules, and Personal Rules. In short, they are rules to guide my thinking and help steer my decision making, and they are just as valuable to me as my business plan. What will the Golden Rules be in your own business?

GOLDEN RULES

Communication and Management Rules

1. **Life is theater; everyone is an actor—some in the lead, some in the supporting cast.**

   This is a metaphor that I came up with one day while trying to verbalize the nature of teamwork. The lead often gets the attention and the accolades, but that does not mean that he or she is more important that the smaller parts who make the play possible. It simply means that each performance has a story that needs to be told and a certain number of characters who have a designated purpose within that story to help to tell it, move it forward, and get it to its conclusion.

   The same is true in the business world. Everyone within a company shares a common goal: create a superior product for the customer and, by doing so, earn a return for the shareholders. However, not everyone can be in the boardroom, nor can everyone be on the showroom floor or on the assembly line or making the sales pitch. It doesn't make any one role more or less important, because each is absolutely necessary to achieve the overall product.

(I think it's helpful to remember, too, that while the lead roles usually get more applause, they are also the ones who tend to get trashed by the critics!)

2. **Never ask a question that you don't already have the answer to.**

I know I dismissed this philosophy in the previous chapter with regard to interview opportunities with mentors so that you can maximize your time. However, this old lawyer trick is one that does have an important place in business. Just as a lawyer does not want to be thrown a curveball in front of the court while examining a witness, a business owner does not want to be caught off guard in front of potential clients or investors. I can remember vividly when I broke this rule in a SkyPipeline board meeting. As the CEO of the company, I asked a question of the board, and I did not know the answer to it. Needless to say, I didn't like the response to my question. Afterward, my attorney, the late Joe Nida, pulled me aside and gave me this Golden Rule.

As a side note to this rule, though, I want to also add this: if you don't know the answer to something, say so.

3. **If you are unsure of the answer to a question, say, "I don't know, but I will get you the answer by [day, time, date]."**

I've seen countless executives in the boardroom (including some of my own, unfortunately) attempt to answer a question they didn't know the answer to, answer a different question, or evade the question altogether. If you don't have 100 percent accurate information or all the details in front of you, just say you don't know. I've made the personal mistake of guessing the answer to an important question, and it has often come back to bite me. One time I was asked where I expected a market to be a year later. I had no idea, but I gave an answer anyway, and my answer was way off. At the next board meeting, the same question came up again, and this time, my answer was totally different. The board noted it, and I noted that I would never answer a question that I didn't have the answer to. You only have one chance to establish credibility. Don't blow it by attempting to have all the answers.

Make sure that you know the ins and outs of your business thoroughly so you have the answers to questions that drive your business. There is nothing more disappointing to an investor than a CEO or a manager who doesn't know his or her core metrics and objectives. Talk to your managers and employees to understand their challenges and concerns. This will not only help you make better decisions for the company and win the respect of your coworkers, but it will also help create confidence with outsiders as you demonstrate the involvement and sweat equity you are willing to put into your business.

4. **"The secret of getting ahead is getting started. The secret of getting started is breaking down your complex overwhelming tasks into small manageable tasks, and then starting on the first one." —Mark Twain**

As I mentioned above with my Connect Four troubles, I have to attack the first things first and worry about everything else down the road. That being said, this quote from Mark Twain offers some of the most valuable advice I have ever encountered. It seems simple enough, but it's often hard to remember when you're facing a mountain of seemingly impossible obstacles with your business. The key is not to view everything as one huge, looming project. Instead, focus on all of the individual elements that make up every bigger challenge, and then prioritize them.

Create a good old to-do list, and start working your way through it. If something seems too daunting to face at the moment, skip it if time and circumstances allow you to, and move on to the next item. When you get through your list, circle back to the beginning, and start over with the projects you passed over the first time around. Each item you are able to check off creates a sense of accomplishment, which in turn creates momentum. But you have to be willing to take that first step, to tackle that first obstacle before you can hope to make any progress on the rest.

In chapter 13, we will discuss the importance of identifying your priorities. Following this strategy, which will help you tackle the first things first, is a key step in making sure that you are able to keep your to-do list in perspective.

5. **When you feel you have failed at something, ask yourself:**

- Why did this happen?

- What could I have done differently?

- How can I do it better next time?

- What changes should I make in my strategies?

- What can I do to improve my planning and preparation?

While it's important to move past our failures and not let them hold us back, it's equally as important to make sure that we learn from them so that we don't repeat our mistakes. I really like the checklist above because it is fairly comprehensive in terms of evaluating the problem while focusing on the positive. It allows me to hold myself accountable without beating myself up. I call this process the postmortem, whereby we go back and evaluate our failures to make sure we learned our lessons so we don't have to repeat them.

I suggest keeping a notebook specifically for lessons you learn the hard way. Take the time to actually record the answer to each question so you have a written reminder of what went wrong and what you resolved to do differently. Share these questions with your employees, too. If your whole team is continually focusing on improvement, failure will be a valuable tool for learning rather than a roadblock in the way of progress.

6. **It's not failure, it's feedback.**

This quote is closely related to number 5. Don't beat yourself up over mistakes. Sure, it's disappointing when you screw up—believe me, I know—but if you focus on the negative instead of the positive, you miss out on a valuable opportunity for growth.

As Thomas Edison famously said, "I have not failed. I've found 1,000 ways that won't work." Use each mistake, each failure, as your springboard to the next step toward achieving your goal.

7. **Become a MASTER OF ACTION.**

To become a "master" of something, you must work with focus and purpose. That is my goal each time I set out on a new project or explore a new industry. I want to master it. I want to immerse myself in it so I can know everything I possibly can about it.

 **Under no circumstances should you communicate negative emotions via e-mail. You never know what's going on with people when they are reading your message, and** you can't know how they will interpret it. Don't leave difficult communication to chance.

But that kind of dedication isn't limited to learning. I also strive to become a master of action—someone who is never content to sit by the sidelines but who is always engaged in the process of selling, networking, expanding, negotiating, researching, and exploring. In short, I want to be *doing*. I have resolved never to be content with simply watching my business; I want to be covered in its mud and grease and blood and sweat and tears. If I go down, I'm going to be fighting when I do.

8. **Never express a negative emotion in an e-mail or text message.**

Under no circumstances should you communicate negative emotions via e-mail. These conversations should be had in person or over the phone. John Tolmie, the CFO of ViSalus, has what he calls the 24-hour rule. If he finds a desire to respond emotionally to something going on in the business, he sleeps on it and responds the next day. This is outstanding advice for any business leader.

You can't control how a person will react or under what conditions he or she is reading your message. What if the person you are sending the message to is reading it during significant family stress or after just having lost a loved one—would you still send it? You never know what's going on with people when they are reading your message, and you can't know how they will interpret it. Don't leave difficult communication to chance.

Not only will you come across as more collected and professional, but don't forget that once something is written down, it becomes permanent. Do you really want someone to have a tangible reminder of when you flew off the handle? Always, *always* fight the urge to fire off an angry e-mail or text message. You will not regret your decision.

9. **Praise in public and reprimand in private.**

You'll command the love of your team when you praise them in public and single out individuals for a job well done; however, if you have something critical to say, I highly suggest that you do it in private. Public embarrassment is a sure way to drive people to perform at a lower level. Imagine your fear if every time you made a mistake, you were embarrassed in front of your peers and colleagues—people whom you respect and admire. You would likely stop taking risks or putting in extra effort, and would probably perform only to satisfactory standards. The last thing you want as an entrepreneur is employees who are only satisfactory.

Coach John Wooden lived by this rule, and so does former LSU basketball coach, Dale Brown. Coach Brown once told me the way he would inspire Shaqille O'Neal to perform at a higher level when Shaq was playing college ball. If Coach Brown observed Shaq underperforming, he would pull him aside and say, "When you played Kentucky, you dominated your opponent—he couldn't stop you, Shaq! This guy you are up against is not better than you. You need to play like you did against Kentucky. You are better than this. You are not playing like the Shaq that I know!" But he would never, ever criticize Shaq's playing in front of anyone else.

I learned a lot about how to motivate people just from that simple story. Dale Brown got Shaq to play to a higher standard—a standard that was of his own making. To this day, Shaq credits Coach Brown's mentorship with much of his great success. If you don't learn how to convey disappointment effectively and if you criticize people publicly, you will eventually find that you've driven away your most talented people. But if you can motivate your team in the right way by celebrating accomplishments and quietly addressing shortcomings, you'll have their loyalty and respect.

Business Model Rules

1. **We are a model-driven company. Test our assumptions, and revisit our model routinely. Rip the model apart every time you look at it.**

2. **Create a retention-based sales model; ideally, pay a long-term residual.**

3. **Be as close to your customer as you can be.**

4. **Cherry-pick your new markets.**

5. **Know your customer.**

This combination of statements is a great one for any company of mine because it is full of action words like "test," "rip," and "create." It encourages each employee to get fired up about the product and the market, and it challenges everyone to be a living, energetic force in the growth of the business.

If you are not passionately engaged in the process, how will you ever really understand what it is that you're selling? I want employees who are willing to look critically at the product and who will offer suggestions. I want employees who are constantly looking for ways to improve our offerings and set higher goals. I want employees who care enough to invest themselves by taking an active role in our company's growth.

6. **Marketing exists to create sales.**

It sounds like a fairly self-evident statement, but sometimes it is easy to get wrapped around a promotion or an ad campaign because it is clever or catchy but not necessarily the best way to reach the consumer. Even in a campaign intended to build a brand image, the ultimate goal is to increase sales. The simplicity of this statement is a good reminder to me that marketing, as well as everything within our company's structure, needs to be focused first and foremost on creating sales.

7. **The best formula for increasing sales: Exposure x Conversion = Result**

Essentially, what this formula represents is the effectiveness of your marketing and of your sales force. Exposure is how you let people know about your product. Do you use direct mail? Viral marketing? Traditional media ads in print, radio, and television? Do you use social networking applications? How do you spread the word about what you have to offer, and how effective is each approach? This is what will determine your overall sales numbers.

The goal, of course, is to increase your rate of exposure while increasing the rate of conversion (i.e., how many people actually purchase the product).

Methods of advertising do not yield equal results and can be dependent on any number of outside factors. Internet outreach, for example, can spread the word among young people but is not as effective in an older demographic. And while it can provide great exposure, it does not translate to a very high conversion rate. Direct mail usually only yields about a 2 percent conversion rate. From my experience, radio advertising has a conversion rate of about 0.5 percent, which is not bad, but it depends on what stations you select when determining whether you're able to reach the right demographic. Direct presentations consistently have the highest rate of conversion, but that rate is largely dependent on how skilled your presenter is and how compelling the reasons are to buy now as opposed to later. A good presenter can have a conversion rate of 85 percent; the challenge is that Direct Sales presentations are not always an easy option to arrange with many products.

Whatever the case, this rule is an important one to remember. It is not advertising alone that will increase your sales. A strong and well-researched marketing plan is a crucial part of the formula as you seek to reach potential customers in a manner that is relevant and effective for the sake of making the conversion to sales and getting the results you desire.

 **The best way to separate your business from the pack is to provide customer service at a level that is unmatched by your competitors' services. If you put people instead of profit first, the difference will be apparent to everyone and will increase your sales and your customer loyalty better than any advertising or branding campaign.**

8. **"It is not the strongest species that survive, nor the most intelligent, but the ones most responsive to change." —Charles Darwin**

Put plainly and simply, adaptation is key to survival. Keep abreast of the market trends, and know when it is better to go with them and when it is better to radically depart from them. You need to be able—and willing—to change your game plan when conditions—such as demand, market, or technology—shift. When PathConnect's business model looked like a failure, we realized that we had to shift our focus from white-label social networks to tools creation for brands that are sold directly to consumers. We took our company from a sure failure to great return for investors in a matter of six months, because we adapted to our strongest competitive advantages. Darwin was absolutely right—in the wild world of the jungle (or of business), it really is survival of the most adaptive!

9. **Compensation drives behavior.**

Anytime I see a company struggling, I take a look at its compensations system. Almost inevitably, the rewards are not in place for hard work and aggressive, profitable sales strategies. Everyone in the company needs to feel connected to the company's success, either through profit sharing, recognition, or another type of compensation that motivates and honors dedication to the job and to the company's goals. In chapter 11, we will discuss how to structure just such a plan for your company to take care of your employees and to bring out the best of their abilities for the benefit of everyone.

Customer Rules

1. **Service is the greatest opportunity to differentiate.**

This statement is self-explanatory, but that doesn't make it any less important. I have found, time and time again, that the best way to separate your business from the pack is to provide customer service at a level that is unmatched by your competitors' services. If you put people instead of profit first, the difference will be apparent to everyone and will increase your sales and your customer loyalty better than any advertising or branding campaign you could imagine.

2. **Being people oriented is not an acquired skill.**

Related to the rule above, you either are people oriented or you're not. It's not something your business can "work on." You don't have time for that. It's something you have to have from the get-go and something you have to maintain consistently to build up the kind of reputation you want for your company. Make sure your employees understand this rule from the start; it's much easier to keep something great going than to try to rebuild yourself later to win customers back.

3. **"Don't fear your competitor; they'll never send you money. Fear your customer." —Jeff Bezos**

This rule from the founder, president, and CEO of Amazon.com is a profound piece of advice. Worry about your loyalty to your customer, not your customer's loyalty to you. This is an opposite approach to the common practice in which management spends time attempting to look through the customer's eyes back at the company. I prefer to ask these questions: How loyal are we being to our customers? What decisions are we making in the short-term and long-term that might make our customers feel we are disloyal? How do we treat them in our customer service group? If we outsource customer service, will they feel that we don't care about them? How are we giving more to our most valued customers—the ones who have been with us the longest, spent the most, and given the most feedback? These are the questions to focus on first. If you take care of your customers first, everything else will fall into place.

Strategy Rules

1. **"Any army everywhere is an army nowhere." —Sun Tzu**

Sun Tzu's master work was entitled *The Art of War*, but many of his lessons are no less applicable to the marketplace than they are to the battlefield. An army that is spread out widely may cover a lot of ground, but it loses its effectiveness and its potency because its force is too diluted. The same is true of a company that tries to do too many things instead of concentrating its energy on developing one area to be superior to anything else out there.

A business needs to have a focus. I have found that without a clearly defined specialty (we are a technical support company for small business, we are industrial cleaners, we are a baby boutique for toddlers ages 6 months to 3 years, we are a business accounting firm, etc.), it becomes harder and harder to develop a top-notch product because our vision and our resources are so scattered. This is, in essence, the "do one thing and do it well" philosophy.

2. **"One thing at time, all things in succession. That which grows slowly endures." —J.G. Hubbard**

I love this quote because it reminds me that patience is the key. I might not see returns today or tomorrow, but with the right investment of time and effort, my work will flourish and last. Everything has a time and a place, and every process has a proper order. I can't rush something whose time hasn't come yet; that only creates instability. Instead, I need to remember that the things that develop over time are the ones that are more likely to reflect timeless ideals rather than brief trends or flash-in-the-pan popularity.

3. **Keep your friends close, but keep your enemies closer.**

It's an old expression, but it is a sound philosophy. Abraham Lincoln lived by it. So does Bill Gates. Rather than allowing yourself to get sucked into a perpetual battle with your competitors, see if there isn't a way to bring them into the fold. Lincoln brought them into his executive cabinet. Bill Gates gave them jobs at Microsoft. If there is someone out there with enough talent to pose a threat to your business, you might want to consider hiring him or her. After all, wouldn't you rather have that know-how and energy working *for* you than against you?

4. **"Most things wired will become wireless, and most things wireless will become wired." —Nicholas Negroponte**

In what has famously come to be known as the "Negroponte Switch," Nicholas Negroponte, cofounder of the MIT Media Lab, made a startling and prophetic prediction that the technology industry would undergo a tremendous change as advances, functions, and needs developed.

When he first made this pronouncement, people thought it was absurd, but he was quickly proved correct. To me, this symbolizes a man who was so intimately involved in the industry and so deeply ingrained in its inner workings that nothing escaped his notice, including inevitable (if seemingly unlikely) future trends.

As we will discuss further in chapter 12, anyone who hopes to be successful in his or her field must become a student of the industry. You have to understand not only where the field has been, but also where current trends and projected advancements are going to take it two, five, ten, or twenty years down the road. That degree of knowledge constitutes wisdom in the business world, and wisdom is one of the most valuable resources any individual can hope to gain.

5. **Drive your potential customers toward you with a compelling offer to take action now.**

You have to spark interest in your product offering. The first step toward making a sale is to reach out and attract attention. Create within your potential consumer a need to know. Try to get the potential customer to ask: Why is this product important for my life? Is it worth my time and money to learn more?

Be prepared with information for consumers who take that next step of asking questions and gathering information. Take the time to address their inquiries, concerns, and curiosity. This establishes a positive pattern of customer-focused service right from the beginning.

Of course, it's even better if customers are able to recognize right away how your product or service will be of value to them—and it's in this stage that you ultimately want to reach them, anyway—so take the time to make your advantages and unique offerings clear, recognizable, and prominent. This can help propel the consumer to buy, often bypassing the need for further questions or a longer sales pitch.

 **The key to building and maintaining a loyal customer base is to treat them in a way that demonstrates their value to the company. Listen to their concerns, be generous with your return policy or follow-up visits, and always keep their best interests at the heart of your business.**

Personal Rules

1. **"Keep away from people who try to belittle your ambitions. Small people always try to do that, but the really great make you feel that you, too, are great." —Mark Twain**

More wisdom from Mark Twain—priceless. I believe that greatness is something toward which we should all be striving. That doesn't necessarily mean fame or fortune, but it means satisfaction and fulfillment by maximizing our talents. However, there will always be people who will try to stand in your way as you pursue your goals. Whether it is from spite, ignorance, or jealousy, it doesn't matter. The fact is that you need to steer clear of people who are too shortsighted to recognize your potential—or too bitter to be willing to encourage it. You know you are better than whatever they are willing to allow you (or themselves) to be, so don't let them hold you back.

2. **"If you look for the bad in people, you shall surely find it." —Abraham Lincoln**

This is another truism that Lincoln embodied, and I think it's very applicable to what I believe about viewing the world, which necessarily affects how I run my companies.

The fact is, there are many people with some really terrible philosophies, unscrupulous practices, and irresponsible approaches to doing business. It can be discouraging as a business owner to interact with such people and to see how they poison the well for others.

By keeping this quote close to me, I remind myself of two important things. First, there will always be bad people in the world. It is up to me to decide who I will associate with. And second, I can let the sad truth of that weigh me down, or I can choose to change my perspective by instead striving to see and serve the good in people.

I want my employees to have a positive outlook, and I want them to trust the customer. Any consumer knows when he or she is being treated with respect versus being treated with contempt, suspicion, or apathy. The key to building and maintaining a loyal customer base is to treat them in a way that demonstrates their value to the company. Listen to their concerns, be generous with your return policy or follow-up visits, and always keep their best interests at the heart of your business.

3. **"There is no finish line." —Bob Goergen**

Bob Goergen, chairman of Blyth Inc. and the man for whom the Goergen Entrepreneurial Management Program at the University of Pennsylvania's Wharton School of Business is named, gave me this nugget of advice when he bought my company, and it has completely changed my perspective. He explained that establishing and growing a company is not about the end result—when you can retire from the business. You need to continually build your business plan toward a finish line, and then go right on past it as if you can't see it at all. That's the only way to succeed—push past every goal you've set and keep working until you bypass the next one, too. If you are focused only on the day when the hard work ends, you'll never reach it.

4. **The only difference between you today and a year from now is the people you know and what you have learned.**

This has been one of the most important rules for my professional life. It reminds me to take advantage of every learning opportunity I possibly can. If I don't, I will never grow as a person or as a business leader.

It is each entrepreneur's responsibility to focus on development, maturity, perspective, and all the other things that go along with becoming a better manager and business owner. As another famous saying goes, "We cannot control what happens to us, but we can control how we respond to it." I believe this with every fiber of my being—what we make of our circumstances defines who we truly are.

Where will you be in one year? What will you have done with the opportunities put in your path? *Carpe diem*—seize the day. Success is up to you!

CHAPTER 10

STARTING YOUR BUSINESS

You've done all the research, preparation, soul -searching, self-evaluation, and legwork. You're ready to take your business plan and your capital and turn it into reality. But where do you start? How do you launch a business that will capture consumer attention as well as market share? What should you make sure to have in place before the doors open?

There are a number of things to consider, as well as a few different approaches that are possible. I recommend that you keep a notebook on hand while you read this chapter, and jot down ideas as you consider the way you plan to package your company and the public face you want to put out there. If you are able to manage a successful launch, you will be in better shape for securing your next round of funding, so this phase is critical.

The first thing to consider is something you will certainly have looked at before this point, but it's worth discussing here anyway. The way you start your business will depend a great deal on the type of entrepreneurship you have decided to pursue. There are three main options:

A traditional business that you establish from the ground up.

A franchise, wherein you buy the brand and operating procedures of a larger company and operate your own branch of that business.

Direct Sales, in which you are an independent representative or a distributor in a company that creates products or services. As an entrepreneur within a bigger company, you build your own network of distributors and customers based upon the products or services of the company you represent.

Each model has its advantages and disadvantages. For example, a traditional business will allow you to create something based entirely on your own vision, but it does have a higher start-up cost. A franchise can be a great option if you want to bring a recognized product to a specific market and have the weight of a much bigger company behind you in terms of advertising, brand recognition, and established practices. Franchise start-up costs can range from the easily affordable to much higher costs for premium products in high-demand markets. Franchising is not always the best option for someone who is particularly independent and wants the freedom to change company procedures or expand product offerings as the need or opportunity arrives. Direct Sales has the lowest start-up cost of the three options and can offer part-time income opportunities, if a person isn't ready to commit to the full-time needs of a traditional business or doesn't feel he or she has the perfect idea to start a company; however, there isn't the exclusivity of distributors within a geographic area the way there usually is with a franchise. I've personally worked with entrepreneurs that chose Direct Sales and made millions with it. This route is ideal for entrepreneurs who want time freedom, like to help people, are passionate about their company's product or service, and want to become business owners without the large initial capital investment and risk.

 **Nothing sells better than a new product with a great history describing how it came about or what the entrepreneur went through to get it launched. After all, we love to root for the little guy, right?**

ViSalus is a Direct Sales company, so I happen to be a strong proponent of that business model because I've seen it prove successful for countless people. However, I have started several traditional businesses, as well, and those have proven to be incredibly profitable and rewarding for me, too. The key is finding the right fit for you, your interests, and your resources.

Admittedly, there used to be a stigma attached to Direct Sales because of the unscrupulous practices and trends that some companies embraced. I was a bit leery of it myself when I first heard mention of it. However, I have been in the business world long enough to be able to see how many of these companies are well-run institutions that provide genuine opportunities for people seeking to become real entrepreneurs.

My first exposure to the industry was through the Goergen family, who own the PartyLite company. I was so impressed with how tightly run their business was and how profitable it was, that any preconceived notions I had about Direct Sales were completely changed. There really are a number of reputable and highly lucrative Direct Sales companies. For example, if you enjoy cooking but don't want to deal with the hassles of starting your own catering business, a company like Pampered Chef can give you an outlet for your talents. Similarly, if you enjoy the beauty industry and like making women feel good about themselves, companies like Mary Kay or Avon might be just the right fit. Even within a franchise or a direct selling opportunity, though the product and many of the methods are established by corporate headquarters, there is still an opportunity to build a business that uniquely suits your passion, your lifestyle goals, and your entrepreneurial spirit.

But many people seek to create something that can allow them greater creative control. For some, that means starting a business that is based entirely on their own product goals and methods. But even within a franchise, though the product and methods are established by corporate headquarters, there is still the opportunity to establish a store that provides customers with a pleasant and professional experience. Have you ever lived in a town where there are two of the same fast-food restaurants? Often, one is much more popular than the other because of the culture the franchise owner has created within the establishment. It can be a rewarding experience to hear people say, "We always drive past the other store to come to this one because your employees are more polite, and your restrooms are cleaner." In any of the three types of business—traditional, Direct Sales, or franchise—if you create a business that people are proud to be a part of, you will set yourself up for a customer base that is proud to do business with you.

Again, it is up to you to determine what option appeals the most to your personality, motivations, resources, and goals.

Once you have determined which type of entrepreneurship model is right for you, you need to think about the story of your product. Nothing sells better than a new product with a great history describing how it came about or what the entrepreneur went through to get it launched. After all, we love to root for the little guy, right? A good true story helps build a connection to the person behind the product and connects a face to the brand name, which makes it seem more personal and, therefore, more trustworthy.

Consider Michael Dell. It is impossible to read any article about him without seeing mention of the fact that he used to build computers in his garage when he was still a teenager and that he started a computer company in his dorm room at UT Austin. He now has an estimated net worth of $12.3 billion. Not too shabby. The point is that the story of its founder's climb to the top is an essential part of the Dell brand. We inherently feel admiration for someone who created something so huge literally from the work of his own two hands.

The same is true with the dietary supplement Airborne. Its story went viral (no pun intended). Everyone seemed to know it was developed by a schoolteacher who was tired of catching every bug that was going around. Her name is Victoria Knight-McDowell, and she started to test vitamin and herbal mixtures to see what combination would provide the strongest boost to the immune system. She began selling her product to small, local drugstores. Next, it was picked up by a national specialty shop; then Walmart and other mainstream stores began to carry it, and within a few years, it was everywhere! The company now does over $500 million a year in sales.

There is just something compelling about a company that was started from sheer ingenuity in pursuit of a solution to a very practical problem. That's the kind of hook you want your company to have; that's the buzz you want to create about your product. Which is a more intriguing product? One that comes from a box store with some brand name slapped on it, or one that was developed by a single mother who was laid off and who, in an effort to provide for her family, built up a successful company with a popular line? Whom would you rather support? A national franchise, or a local guy who got fed up with his boss and started his own company with the vision of offering superior service?

What is your story? What makes your company simultaneously sympathetic and empowering? Stories like Michael Dell's and Victoria Knight-McDowell's grab us because they play to the fantasy of striking out on our own and actually succeeding. Remember, of the millions who dream of doing it, very few people ever actually make that leap into entrepreneurship. Stories like these that surround products appeal to our dream of maybe someday having the guts to do something similar ourselves.

One of the biggest mistakes I hear from entrepreneurs is that they don't want anyone to know their humble origins because they think it will hurt the public perception of their company's credibility and stability. While this can be a valid concern—and we will discuss how to counter that later in this chapter—I would encourage you to celebrate whatever it is that got you to this point, and to make sure others know about it, too. Everyone loves an underdog story. Feel free to embrace your own.

Are you an ex-salesperson for IBM who marveled at the inefficiencies of certain software, so you invented a product to solve the problem? That's perfect! Are you a stay-at-home mom who was struck by the lack of heirloom-quality children's clothing in your area, so you decided to launch your own boutique? Great—that makes me want to learn more about you and your company.

But what is the best way to get that story out there? Other than your friends and family, who else is likely to be bragging about your efforts? How do you spread the word about your business to obtain that word-of-mouth promotion? There are two main things you need to get started: a good Web site and a good name.

First, the Web site. It's quite simple: every business, no matter how small, no matter what, should have a Web site. They are cheap, easy to develop, and easy to get going. There are almost certainly a number of Web development companies in your area with whom you can partner to construct a professional-looking site that provides basic, essential information about your company, including location (if you have a brick-and-mortar storefront), hours, product or service descriptions, contact information, customer service guarantee, and your story. Make it easy to navigate and clean in appearance, and you'll be miles ahead of your nondigital competition.

It may seem like an added expense or a detail that can be addressed when you're a little more established, but don't fall into that thinking. It's absolutely essential to have a site up and running before you open your doors. Without a Web site, you will be deemed a Luddite, an amateur, a person who is out of touch. You will be perceived as strapped for cash because you couldn't afford one, and even if things are very tight financially, as a business owner you cannot ever create a perception of lack of a money—no matter what. Even if you don't have money, and even if you have no clients, you must never let that image be apparent to your customers because it creates unease and a lack of consumer confidence in you. Invest in your Web site. When reviewing a prospective business, I find that if their Web site isn't high quality and professional-looking, I will immediately lose interest. Sometimes new entrepreneurs are pennywise and pound foolish. Don't fall into that trap. It will cost you customers, prospective investors, and employees.

A small investment up front in a solid Web site will not only give you an extra boost of professionalism, but from a practical perspective, it will also save you a great deal of time answering phone calls from people who want to know hours, directions, and offerings.

The second part of getting your story out there and in people's minds as your business launches is having a great name for your company. We talked about the importance of finding the right name when we discussed creating your business plan, but I want to revisit the point here because this is where it really comes into play. If you have a good name, it will stick with people, which does as much to give you brand recognition as does a catchy jingle or slick logo.

Take, for example, Airborne. It's got a great story and a compelling hook, but it also has an extremely smart name. The maker chose a word that has meaning, since many cold viruses are spread through the air. We human beings hate the thought of somebody sneezing in our proximity; we'll hold our breath or try to breathe in the other direction—especially in an enclosed area like an airplane or a classroom. So the product name plays to the common fear, but it gives it a positive spin—it's a way to fight back against the common airborne illnesses we all dread. It's catchy and simple and easy to remember, which makes it able to be duplicated.

The selection of your name should be something that helps tell your story so it sparks continued interest in your product. Think about Google. It wasn't just selected because it's a funny-sounding word; it is the mathematical term for an unimaginably large number—a one with one hundred zeros after it. That's a smart name. It sounds unique so it sticks with you, but it also has a relevant meaning and clues you into something to do with the product or company itself.

 **Figure out how you want to be perceived in the marketplace, and then determine how your name, logo, and branding can work together to promote that.**

But as I stressed before, don't reach for a clever name that is going to feel forced or cause people to roll their eyes at the mention of your business. The most important thing is that your company's title has some kind of significance, a reason why it is called what it is called. In other words, the name should be tied to your story. This will help with your marketing, branding, and public perception.

Some people want to have their name in the title, like "Thompson & Sons Furniture Company." That is a fine option, too, if you are creating something you want to be your legacy as a family-owned-and-operated company. If that name is part of the value of your company—if you are willing to stake your personal reputation on the quality of your products—then by all means go in that direction. Just make sure that your reasoning is part of the story.

Don't allow your business name to be perceived as ego driven—your name up there simply because you want the world to know you're successful. Instead, use your Web site and company literature to explain how the company was founded on the concept of the ideology and philosophies of the family for which it was named. Avoid using "I" or "we" in this description because, again, you want to avoid sounding ego driven or self-serving. Instead, write up your story in the third person so that it connects the customer to your ideals instead of your personal pride.

Now, I know that some people are a little leery of having a name that reveals the company to be a family-based business because they fear the perception of being a small-time operation. I firmly believe, however, that we are in the midst of a major trend that is orienting toward family-run companies. Most of us would rather support a locally owned business than a global corporation—we want to keep our money in the area and give our business to the people who have stuck their necks out and worked hard to establish a reputation here in our community. I think a lot of this is tied to Americans' natural tendency to side with the little guy, but I think it also has to do with some of the major news stories over the past number of years concerning companies like Enron and various Ponzi schemes. There isn't necessarily safety in size anymore. Corporate greed disgusts us, and as our confidence is shaken by stories of unethical and hugely harmful practices, I believe that the value of face-to-face service and accountability will continue to grow in the minds of the consumers.

 **I suggest that you use the word "we" instead of "I," even if you are the only person in your company for the moment. By using the word "we," you can help create a sense of confidence that your business really is more substantial than a small organization just starting to get off the ground.**

As you look to develop your primary marketing plan, take all of these issues into account. Whatever direction you've decided to take with the name of your business, you will need to calculate a strategy to help get that name out into the marketplace and your reputation for trustworthiness in people's minds.

The same designer whom you hire to work on your Web site may also be able to help you put together a professional-looking logo. Focus on clean lines and a limited number of colors. This makes it simpler to reproduce and gives you a color palette from which you can work when designing the rest of your materials. Think about school colors and sports teams. With two or three colors, they are able to establish a kind of brand recognition. Try to be consistent with these colors in your advertising, company literature, and labels.

Keep in mind, too, that you want to make it clear what kind of industry you are in. Give your company a clear identity so its name will become synonymous with the product or service you are offering. Figure out how you want to be perceived in the marketplace, and then determine how your name, logo, and branding can work together to promote that.

If you're in a Direct Sales company, you would be creating a team name instead of a company name. For instance, to use an example from ViSalus, one of the distributors named their team the Generational Wealth Builders. They've successfully branded themselves and their team within the company.

Next, create a pitch that helps people understand exactly what your place is within the industry. For example, if you provide standardized-test tutoring for students, the big industry is education, but the specialization is test preparation. Anyone who reads your literature or checks out your Web site should know exactly who your target demographic is—in this case, college-prep students and the parents of those students.

Building off this, you should also make sure that your marketing plan clearly identifies who you are *not*. Commonly, one of the biggest mistakes new businesses make with their marketing is trying to reach too broadly to capture every possible facet of their industry. While it's great to have broad vision, don't let your company develop an identity crisis.

Use your "what we're not" statement as a positive attribute for creating your brand image. If your business is test preparation, then try including a sentence or two that says, "This is not a program intended to amuse students or to help them finish their homework more easily. Ours is a rigorous program designed for focused and intensive SAT/ACT preparation for university-bound students." With that sentence, you are immediately making a statement that identifies your target as students and parents with serious interest and high expectations. It demonstrates that you are passionate about working with people who are also passionate, and it implies that parents can feel good about getting their money's worth.

There is another thing to consider with regard to how you present yourself, though, and it has nothing to do with your marketing plan. It has to do with how you represent yourself in your own speech and how you present your role within the company—and the two are very closely linked.

First, I suggest that you use the word "we" instead of "I," even if you are the only person in your company for the moment. While it is true that there is a resurgence of confidence in and loyalty to small businesses, there is still a sense of security that the consumer feels when he or she goes with a larger company. Because it has been around longer, it feels more established and thus less likely to have closed its doors by the time they need maintenance or service. By using the word "we," you can help create a sense of confidence that your business really is more substantial than a small organization just starting to get off the ground.

This is an important tip for dealing with potential clients as well as potential investors. Whenever investors are dealing with people who represent small businesses, and the investors know there is only one person behind the company, they tend to be less secure in their feelings toward the company. It becomes more difficult for the business owner because the investor holds the leverage, sizing the company up as a smaller competitor with a tiny market share, and therefore less likely to earn a large profit. It may not seem fair, but this is a very real part of business deals.

From my own experience as an angel investor, I know that I am far more likely to invest with a company that engages me by using "we" than one that uses "I," even if both companies have been around for the same amount of time and do comparable sales. When a business owner uses the word "we," I feel more confident, even if I know that there are only a couple of people running it. Use of the word "we" conveys a sense of assurance that the company is going to grow, and it creates a connection between the owner and the client. "We" sounds like a partnership, like we're in this thing together. That makes an investor, and a customer, feel good.

The other thing to consider is your own title within the organization. If you are the founder of the company, it seems logical that you would be the president or CEO. However, you may want to consider bypassing that title until your company becomes a little bit more established. The reasoning behind this is the same as using "we" to discuss your company. If you are the only person in your company for the time being, or even if you have a few other employees, a potential client or investor is going to discern very quickly that you are a very small company and may make any number of unfair judgments about your company as a result.

Once your company has grown a bit and established solid footing within the market, you should feel free to use whatever title you choose. But in the earliest days, it may be advisable to print a slightly less impressive title on your business cards for the sake of creating a stronger impression.

For example, when I launched 24/7 Tech, I chose the company's name because I thought it conveyed a sense of our mission, which was to provide around-the-clock service. The domain name was available, so I purchased that immediately and set about designing our Web site. I did a little research to find out who owned the phone number 877-247-TECH and negotiated a very cheap deal (under $100) with the owner to buy the number, since he was not using it. I went to a design company and had a logo created for the company.

 **It is essential that you always have your pitch articulated so you are able to communicate clearly to any potential customer what you represent as a company and who you are as the person providing them with a product or a service.**

I was incredibly proud of all of my start-up legwork, but instead of insisting on the CEO title I had earned, I wanted to be a vice president. I knew that if I walked into someone's office as a young man and said I was the CEO, he or she would know this was a very new and small operation before I even started my pitch. Many clients will be a little suspicious if the CEO sits down and talks with them at their first meeting, because that implies that either the company is just getting started and is, therefore, a risky gamble or that the company is desperate, which gives the other person all of the power in the negotiations.

However, by the time I exited 24/7 Tech and established SkyPipeline, I had a few more years under my belt, not to mention a lot more experience. I had a few newspaper and magazine articles to my name, and I had a reputation as an up-and-coming entrepreneur. Because of that, even though we were still a small company, I felt I could take over the CEO title without giving investors the impression that we were too small or too new to be taken seriously.

My sales angle was different, too. I made sure that potential clients understood the positive aspect of working with the company I was heading. At some point in each sales pitch, I'd ask them, "When was the last time the CEO of AT&T, MCI, or Verizon showed up to actually talk to you about working on an account with them?" The answer was always that it never happened, because the companies were too big to operate that way.

"It's not that they're too big to meet with you," I'd explain. "It's that they are too big to provide one-on-one, personalized service." I would give clients my cell phone number and tell them they could call me anytime. That was my first step in assuring them that we would provide customer service unlike anything they had ever had before.

It is essential that you always have your pitch articulated so you are able to communicate clearly to any potential customer what you represent as a company and who you are as the person providing them with a product or a service. Don't make it sound scripted or overrehearsed, but do have a clear sense of how you want to present yourself as you go out to make sales calls, and figure out how to best convey that in a manner that will invoke confidence in your business.

My final piece of advice for starting your business is to sell first and ask questions later. In other words, if you have a product or service that is ready to go, and you have customers already lining up to purchase it, don't delay until you have every detail firm with your incorporation contract or your Web site. Go ahead and sell! That's the whole point of everything else you're working on, anyway.

 **Word of mouth is far and away one of the most effective forms of advertising there is. If you win over your earliest customer with your service, integrity, and hard work, your reputation will precede you as you get deeper and deeper into the market.**

What most small businesses don't realize is that one can register as a sole proprietor and start selling tomorrow. Then you can worry about opening your bank account. With every company I've ever started, the time that I registered it and did all my legal work was when I already had my first check in hand. To open your bank account, you have to be incorporated and be doing business as such, so I always went and sold the first deal. That forced my hand to actually do all the other work.

Obviously, it's best to have as many things in place as possible before you launch your business, but never let a deal go simply because you don't have things in exactly the order you want them. You can work that out as you go if you need to. Your first sales are something you need to pounce on.

If I were to have an entrepreneur show up to my office looking for mentorship advice about how to set all the necessary pieces and he were to say, "I've got 100 orders and no idea how to legally incorporate," that's not just someone whom I want to mentor, it's someone with whom I want to invest!

This is true for almost any kind of company—service-related companies, shops, and any small business in which the founder has nothing to lose. The possible exception would be someone like an engineer who left Microsoft and who wants to reinvent video on the Web. If it is a product that will take a while to develop, then obviously you can't start selling right away, although you may be able to begin taking advance orders for receipt upon product launch.

Not only is the "sell first, ask questions later" approach a solid one, but if you find yourself fortunate enough to be in that position, it also helps eliminate one of the most frustrating remarks that a new entrepreneur often hears: "I don't want to be the first to buy your product. I want to be the second." People want the confidence of knowing they are not stepping into the complete unknown when they make a purchase.

Unfortunately, not everyone is going to be lucky enough to be in such a successful position right off the bat, and you may find yourself faced with the "I want to be the second buyer" attitude. If that is the case, try to have an answer crafted that addresses the issue while assuaging the fear. For example, if someone asks to see your client list before you have one, you could perhaps answer like this: "Let me tell you about my past work experience and the projects I've worked on to really give you an idea as to how my knowledge and understanding is going to be able to maximize this project's effectiveness for you." That lets the potential client know he or she can trust you to do the job because of your relevant experience, and you don't have to come right out and say, "I've never done this before on my own."

You may be asked point-blank, however, if you have any other accounts lined up. If you do not, you need to be honest and tell them that this would be your company's first sale. You can explain how this could actually work to your client's advantage, though, by saying, "We are a new business, and we want you to be our first client. That means we are going to work twice as hard for you. I can offer you a money-back guarantee or whatever it takes to serve you because, as our first client, we'd like to leverage your testimony and help establish our reputation as the hardest-working company in the business. How does that sound to you?" People admire honesty, aggression, passion, and commitment. If you lead with that, people are going to take you seriously.

In the end, as you start your business and take those first steps, you may feel as if the odds are stacked against you. But the truth is that you can successfully navigate your way through the challenges and trials of getting established if you prepare yourself and your business with a smart, calculated marketing plan that will create a buzz around your company, your story, and even you as a salesperson. Word of mouth is far and away one of the most effective forms of advertising there is. If you win over your earliest customer with your service, integrity, and hard work, your reputation will precede you as you get deeper and deeper into the market.

That first day of business can often be the most frightening, but if you have nothing to lose, you will find it exhilarating, too, as you throw open the doors to your new business and your new life.

CHAPTER 11

GROWING, HIRING, AND FIRING

Business is booming. Your accounts are expanding, your client list is growing, the profits are increasing, and the demand is starting to exceed what you can handle without bringing on some additional assistance. How does a small business navigate through the often-tricky realm of recruiting, compensating, and maintaining quality people?

It's a rather complex issue with a variety of options that may or may not be suited for your business, depending on the nature of your industry and the chemistry of your workforce. What we discuss here will hopefully give you a starting place from which to evaluate your needs and your resources and to begin constructing a plan that will work best for your business. It can be trial and error sometimes as you try to determine the right solution for your current situation, but my hope is that after reading this chapter, you will have a set of ideas that will make you feel empowered and confident as you strive to meet the needs of your company and your employees.

The hiring process can be scary. It's taking a huge risk because suddenly you're extending the boundaries of your company beyond just you and your family, and you are trusting someone else with a part of what you've created.

I've seen businesses fail because they didn't hire people when they should have; on the other hand, I've seen businesses suffer because they hired the wrong person for the job. The best piece of advice that I can offer as you start the hiring process for the first time is to know what kind of employee you are looking for.

In most cases, when a small business is making its first few hires, you are not seeking a person with highly specialized training, but rather someone who can do a little bit of everything—a kind of jack-of-all-trades. You need someone who will be willing to work the phones, take out the trash, interact with customers, and mop the floor—in other words, anything that will allow you more time to make sales calls and handle accounts will be part of the new employee's job description.

 **The value of association is a powerful thing— if you surround yourself with tremendous talent, you will find yourself challenged and stretched to levels you never imagined. Aim as high as you can when hiring a new employee.**

You need to make sure that the person you hire is willing to accept that kind of position. Some people are adamant about what they are and are not willing to do as part of a job. If someone thinks dusting the shelves or refilling the paper towels in the bathroom is beneath him or her, then you don't want that person. Make it clear to the employee that everyone involved with your business has a responsibility to pitch in and to take care of whatever needs to be done so the company can make a good impression on its customers while meeting their needs.

The first position I have created with any of my businesses has always been this type of an office manager role. In fact, that was usually how I listed the job when I advertised it. I wanted someone who was interested in managing with a sense of responsibility, because that gives him or her a personal connection to the company. In each interview, I would look for someone who took initiative and seemed to be on the lookout for whatever job might need doing. That kind of person tends to take pride in his or her work, which is exactly the kind of attitude I wanted in my company.

When the time comes and you are ready to hire for highly specialized positions, you should still keep this kind of attitude in mind. The employee needs to have a definite job description and a clear set of expectations; but you should also explain that from time to time, he or she may be called upon to step outside of that description to help with a project or situation that is part of the company's growth.

Ideally, you want a candidate who will readily accept this kind of job flexibility. He will be committed to the position for which he is hired and will understand that ultimately, everyone is working for the good of the company, and that may mean pitching in, in a slightly different manner when extra hands are needed. People who are overly protective or territorial about their job description tend not to be team players. You want someone who is concerned with doing good work for the sake of the customer, product, brand, and company, not someone who is just hacking away at a job strictly for a paycheck.

I've always believed that my most valuable assets are the quality of people I've been able to attract and recruit to my companies. The value of association is a powerful thing—if you surround yourself with tremendous talent, you will find yourself challenged and stretched to levels you never imagined. It is my goal, therefore, to be in awe of every person I hire. I want to see traits in him or her that are more dynamic or more positive than my own abilities in that area. Because I know that simply by working with that person, I will be able to grow, and the company will prosper, thanks to this continual reach for improvement.

The best advice I can offer when hiring a new employee is to aim as high as you can. Some people caution against hiring overly qualified applicants because they are more likely to leave for another job or require a higher salary. But if you have created a work environment that is nurturing and encouraging, most people will opt to stay put rather than make a few extra dollars somewhere that has a miserable team and bad morale. And don't be afraid of the higher salary if you know the person is the right one for the job. I once hired a CFO at a rate significantly more than I was making. Sure, that was slightly humbling as the CEO, but I knew this individual was the best person for the job, and I was so eager to bring his talents, perspective, experience, and leadership on board that I was willing to pay whatever it took. I knew that it was an investment in the growth of our company. I never regretted that decision.

You want people who will take a personal interest in the job, and you want the right people for the position. Those traits are key, no matter what level you're looking to hire. As you start to expand your business and pull together an actual team of employees, you need to consider the team dynamic and think about what kind of players you need to make that team successful. And I'm not only talking about what kind of skills people have to offer; I'm talking about creating the right chemistry.

When you can bring together a group of people who work well together and feed off one another's energy and ideas, you will not only have the advantage of a strong and talented workforce, you will also have happy employees—and employee contentment is one of the biggest factors in retaining people, recruiting more people, and increasing productivity.

However, to obtain—and maintain—that kind of chemistry, you have to be very selective about whom you bring on board. A person who brings a condescending air, any kind of perceived laziness, or a hostile attitude to the group can completely destroy the positive atmosphere you've worked so hard to create.

I watched one particular business absolutely crumble in a fairly short period of time because the boss continually brought on the cheapest help he could hire, whether that person fit with his established team or not. He never took the time to screen people for the right attitude, work ethic, or personality that would accentuate and add to the talent he already had with his company.

I sat down with John Wooden to learn how he put together the incredible teams that he did. He wasn't into recruiting the hottest, most headline-grabbing players out there; instead, he researched each potential recruit carefully to learn how that player would fit in with his team. When he or his assistants went on visits, they would carefully observe the young man's behavior, not only toward his teammates, but toward his parents—was he respectful? They would look to see how he interacted with the maintenance staff—did he quickly move out of the way when someone was mopping the court, or did he make the person work around him? How did he leave his area of the locker room—was it a mess he just expected that someone else would handle, or did he take responsibility for his own belongings and clean up after himself?

All of these factors were part of the recruiting process for Coach Wooden because he wanted to make sure that he was going after only the players who would enhance the chemistry of the UCLA basketball team rather than break it down with a negative attitude or disruptive personality.

I really take this lesson to heart when I prepare to hire someone. As I write up the position posting, I try to take a similar kind of thoughtful approach about what kind of person I want to recruit for my team. In fact, sometimes I even ask myself how the FBI would handle it if they were trying to profile someone for this job, and then I tailor the ad around that. I want to have as clear a picture as I can about the kind of people I'm intending to bring on board. I want to know how they view themselves, how they interact with others, how they perceive their role within the company, what schools they went to, and why they chose those schools. I really want to understand the personality, motivation, and worldview of the person I am hiring, because that is going to have an impact on everyone else in the company.

 **Evaluate your applicants based not only on their capabilities, but also on how their personality will fit in with the company. You want the new employee to be comfortable with the ones already on staff and to be able to blend with them in a way that not only complements what you've already got but also gives the new hire a chance to exercise his or her unique skill set, talents, or perspective.**

Obviously, you would not hire someone based on things like political views or religious beliefs. Not only is that a violation of nondiscrimination laws, it's also not ethical. You have to be careful not to ask too many personal questions regarding age or family status. You may think that you are simply being friendly, but it will be worth your time to do a little research to determine what kind of specific questions are and are not legally permitted as part of an interview.

But you do want to make sure that you evaluate your applicants based not only on their capabilities, but also on how their personality will fit in with the company. You want the new employee to be comfortable with the ones already on staff and to be able to blend with them in a way that not only complements what you've already got but also gives the new hire a chance to exercise his or her unique skill set, talents, or perspective.

One screening technique I use is the Connect Four board I keep on my desk. I will often challenge a potential applicant to play me in a round, which enables me to observe a number of things about the person. Not only do I see how he or she calculates strategy, but I also get a chance to learn about his or her level of competitiveness and sportsmanship. If a person has a chance to beat me and chooses not to take it, I am not interested in bringing him on board. I want someone who isn't afraid to challenge me, who is willing to assert her point of view if it will result in the most favorable outcome. Likewise, if someone is a poor sport, either through being overly competitive and taking a loss badly, or by becoming overly aggressive during play, followed by a gloating win, I also don't want that person as part of the team.

I strive for balance and camaraderie in my companies, and if someone's personality risks throwing that into jeopardy, I will not even consider hiring him or her. And I'm not alone. Every mentor and business leader I have ever spoken with has cited the quality of their team as the reason for their success. Nothing is worth risking that team balance.

For me, commitment and loyalty are incredibly important. If the employee seems to jump from job to job to job, continually chasing the bigger, better deal, I'm not interested. Sometimes, of course, a person has several "blips" on his résumé as a result of something else, so I want to make sure to give him a fair shake if he meets the qualifications. But I'm always on the lookout for people who match my image of how the ideal job candidate will act.

 **If a person simply is not fitting in with your company in such a way that he or she is detrimental to your team, you need to let that employee go immediately. It's not pleasant, and it's not easy, but it is necessary to fire people—and you need to get comfortable with that reality very quickly.**

You need to go with your gut when making hiring decisions. If the person just doesn't feel like the right fit, he or she probably isn't. Trust your instincts in this regard—I've ignored mine in the past and made some horrible hiring choices that cost millions. Put a price tag on a new hire: Is it worth the $50,000 or $100,000 if he or she becomes a fully productive employee? What if the employee doesn't work out? How much will it end up costing me, if this is the wrong person, once I take into account salary costs, disruption in the office, lost sales, re-advertising, and rehiring someone new? Often, hiring the wrong person can be a $100,000-plus mistake.

Look for warning signs that the candidate might represent your company in a negative light with clients. Some of the worst mistakes I've made in hiring have come when I ignored my instincts and hired someone who seemed careless or not genuinely interested in the company. I have hired people who were overly casual, who used slang or even crass language in interviews. That has always proven to be a mistake. I pay attention to whether they speak badly about former coworkers or bosses. Sometimes, though, I have rationalized hiring a person who goes against those professional traits I hold so important, and it always comes back to haunt me.

Luckily, there are a few ways to rectify hiring mistakes. One is by relocating the person to a different area in the company. For example, if I hire someone to handle my customer accounts and I find that his job skills really aren't a good match for that position—in fact, I would never hire him for this same position, knowing what I know now—I can simply restructure his position if he is a good worker whom I would like to keep with the company. I can look to see if there is a better match for his talents or experience somewhere else in the company, so that I can retain his talent and loyalty, but in a position that both of us will be probably be happier with. Maybe he is better at operations; if so, I would slide him over there and start looking for a new customer accounts manager.

If, however, the person simply is not fitting in with your company in such a way that he or she is detrimental to your team, you need to let that employee go immediately. It's not pleasant, and it's not easy, but it is necessary to fire people—and you need to get comfortable with that reality very quickly. I've hired and fired hundreds of people, and I have learned that you have to look at it as a necessity for the life of your business.

Firing is one of the most important things for a growing business. You should think of it as pruning a plant—you don't want its resources to continue to go toward branches and leaves that aren't producing anything. Instead, you need to trim them off right away so the finely manicured result is something that maximizes its resources in the most effective way for the overall health of the organism. And you need to cut the wrong people out quickly. A bad employee is a cancer for your company that spreads and damages the entire body. The sooner you remove the problem, the better.

You need to call the employee into your office and explain how he or she is not living up to the expectations of the position. It is incredibly helpful if you have job report evaluations from supervisors or even ones you've completed on your own, in which you have expressed your displeasure in the individual's performance on previous occasions. It is important that you are communicating with your employees and that they know when they need to improve before the ax falls.

If you have had a frank and honest evaluation of your employee's performance previously, you will have had the chance to explain, "When I hired you, I thought you were the right fit for this job; but since then, I have come to see that your [communication skills or work ethic or attitude or judgment] is not up to par. If things do not improve, I will have to let you go for the sake of the company." By communicating your expectations to the employees before the point of needing to fire them, you are not only giving them an opportunity to change their ways, but you are also making sure that you have a clear record of poor employee performance should one of those people choose to challenge your decision to finally let him or her go.

When it turns out that you did make a mistake with your hiring choice, and the situation is such that the individual must be fired, take care of doing so swiftly. Do not hold on to the individual simply because you are too uncomfortable with the prospect of firing him or her. Do what you need to do, knowing that it is the best thing to preserve this business you have created.

Just remember that hiring and firing the right employees is probably the most important thing that you can do. Ask yourself a question about each employee: If he or she were to come to you and say, "I am leaving your company for a new opportunity," what would your gut reaction be? Would you be devastated because this person's contribution is invaluable and irreplaceable, or would you be happy because by leaving he or she would eliminate many problems and open up an opportunity for someone more qualified? This is a lesson I learned from Jim Collins's excellent book, *From Good to Great: Why Some Companies Make the Leap . . . and Others Don't*, and it has proved invaluable.

As you evaluate each employee, consider whether you would hire him or her again for that same position, knowing what you know now. If the answer is no, then you should seriously look at either moving that person to a more suitable place within the company or letting the employee go. Your business cannot afford to suffer from your indecision.

Moving beyond hiring and firing, let's now consider how to maintain workplace satisfaction among the strong team of employees you have assembled. Always remember this simple truth: compensation drives behavior.

As you hire employees, think carefully about how you'll compensate them. Create a company in which employees go home happy. It not only generates loyalty toward you and your business, but improved morale improves productivity and can even help recruit more quality workers.

If your assets are limited, you may find yourself looking for someone with less experience who will not expect as high a salary. On the other hand, you may be willing to pay a higher price to bring on board someone with a proven track record and relevant experience and education. Sometimes you will find a great cross between the two—someone who has experience but is looking for part-time work or who is willing to take a pay cut to be in a job he or she will love. Whatever the case, you will want to make sure that your new employee is a go-getter, someone who is self-motivated and excited about an opportunity to prove himself or herself in your company.

There are a variety of compensation plans that you can consider, and it will really depend on your resources, the nature of your work, and the employee pool that you have as to which plan—or combination of plans—will be best suited for your company.

The most obvious starting point is salary. As we discussed previously, you may have to find a balance between paying the rate you can afford and hiring someone of the proven quality that you need. You should always be up front about the salary offer so that if an applicant is not interested in the range you have established, you can both look elsewhere and save each other a great deal of time.

 **Meet with your employees to discuss their earning goals and together devise a system that combines the security of salary with the motivation of commission. This can be an effective way of helping your employees as well as your company.**

There are ways to incentivize performance, however, which can supplement a base salary or form the entirety of the compensation, depending on your company. I am, of course, referring to commission. Commission pays the employee a certain percentage of each sale that he or she makes. It is a great way to generate activity and motivate hard work. Unfortunately, it has some catches.

For example, if a higher form of compensation is tied to landing a bigger client, you may find that your employees only pursue those top-dollar accounts. The problem is that, while there may only be ten $10,000 sales out there, there are probably one hundred $1,000 sales. You don't want to miss your smaller opportunities by only going after the large ones.

You can get creative with ways to combat this kind of skewed focus. Something I have tried with one of my teams is pulling out a $100 bill from my wallet and tacking it to the bulletin board in the front of the room. Motion creates emotion, and emotion creates sales. The person who makes the first sale of the day, no matter what size, gets the money. It is great to see people hit the phones hard as a kind of friendly competition grows around who will be the one to claim the prize. Not only does it help generate sales at all levels, but it also creates a sense of pride and accomplishment in whoever does end up winning. That employee has something tangible to bring home and show to his or her spouse and say, "Look at the bonus I earned today."

Another means of compensation that can help promote teamwork is a company-wide bonus. A certain percentage of your profits will be divided among everyone when you all hit your sales goal. An alternate means of doing this is to divide into tiers: employees, managers, and the executive team. Each group has to meet and propose three strategies for increasing performance in their sector. Those in charge of spending money would need to put forward three practical solutions for saving money. Those in charge of making sales would need to propose three new approaches to try. This way, each group has a clear set of goals, with a reward contingent upon how well they are able to hold themselves to those goals over the next month or quarter.

You can also meet with your employees to discuss their earning goals and together devise a system that combines the security of salary with the motivation of commission. This can be an effective way of helping your employees as well as your company.

For example, if you need to make $10,000 per month to cover the cost of one employee's salary, benefits, taxes, and insurance, you need to generate about $20,000 to cover that cost, provided your margins are around 50 percent. You can strike the following deal with that employee: He will earn two-thirds of his monthly salary needs, no matter what, and the remaining third once he hits the required number of sales in the month. That way, the employee has a guaranteed number to count on, a number to shoot for, and the knowledge that both of you are working toward his compensation.

You should always strive to pay fair, market-based wages to recruit and maintain talented, reliable, and loyal employees. I have also incentivized my employees with equity if I want them to be long-term team members with the company. There are multiple ways to issue equity. You can do stair-step vesting, where one earns an increasing amount each year he or she remains with the company. You can do cliff vesting, which means that if an employee stays to a certain point, he or she gets the full amount of an agreed-upon percentage, but forfeits everything if he or she leaves before that point.

You can also do vesting based on deferring market rate wages, which can be a prime way to hire top wage earners if you're not quite in a place to afford them. If someone is worth $100,000, but you can only pay $75,000, you can offer deferred compensation wherein you draw up a contract guaranteeing that when the company hits $5 million dollars (or whatever your goal is), the employee will make ten times his or her deferred income for each year he has stayed with you. This means, for example, that for the employee who defers $25,000 per year and stays with your company for, let's say, four years (when you meet your goal), he or she could potentially earn $25,000 x 10 x 4 years = $1 million! I used this technique at both SkyPipeline and ViSalus. In fact, I once used this deferred compensation plan with my entire start-up team. One executive earned over $300,000 by deferring a mere $25,000 in wages.

Finally, there is a kind of compensation that doesn't cost a cent, but can be every bit as powerful as monetary incentives: recognition, a sense of accomplishment, and a feeling of personal responsibility. Compensation that ties into one of these three areas can be a tremendous motivator.

Recognition is a fundamental human need. People want to be acknowledged. They want the occasional word of encouragement or celebration of their efforts. You can accommodate this in a variety of ways: Employee of the Month programs, letters of commendation for employee personnel files, employee appreciation banquets—the list can go on and on. The point is that people feel a loyalty toward those who recognize their work. As the boss— and especially as your company grows larger—the more you are able to reach out to individuals and show them that they are more than just a profit- generating cog in the machine, the more content a workforce you'll have.

A sense of accomplishment is also significant because people want to know that they are working toward a goal, toward an end. They want to feel that each sale they make, and each customer they reach, means that they are somehow helping build something greater than themselves. Keep your employees informed about how the company is growing and to what end. If you build water purifiers, for example, are you able to donate a certain number each year to villages in India that need fresh drinking water? If you own an industrial cleaning company, do you volunteer your services in disaster-affected areas to help people rebuild their lives? If you run a technology company, are you helping rural communities become wired or assisting after-school programs in the inner city to develop computer classes for the children there?

This kind of corporate goal is incredibly valuable in reminding your workers that what they do really does matter. It's not just earning a paycheck, it's giving back. This is an especially effective form of compensation for those people whose driver is contribution. The sense of accomplishment that they feel when they read about the efforts of the company or when they see photographs of the people their work is helping can be the greatest reward of all and can motivate them to put even more effort in their job.

 **Your product is your people—how they represent your company, how they interact with clients, how they view their own professional lives. You want the highest-quality product you can offer to give your customers the best value.**

And the contribution doesn't have to be that far from home, either. I remember one instance when I was at an employee family dinner, and I looked around at all the little children who were laughing and playing and having a wonderful time. And then it hit me—I have a responsibility to them. I have a personal responsibility to keep this company up and running and generating business because that is what is putting food on their table at home, what is buying them school supplies and warm clothes for the winter. Reminders like that can be tremendous motivators that give perspective and meaning to every decision you make and every sale you pursue. Remember why you're doing it, and don't be afraid to remind your employees, either. When you all share a goal like that, the results can be tremendous.

As you enjoy the growing success of what you have built, keep in mind the variety of ways that you can compensate and reward the people who have helped to get you to this point. Finances can be a tricky topic, but if you concentrate on bringing the right people to your team and creating an atmosphere of motivation, encouragement, and appreciation, you will find that your employee satisfaction rate is one of your company's most valuable assets. Most people would rather work for a little less money and be surrounded by good people in a positive environment. That does far more to heighten the quality of one's life than does a slightly larger paycheck.

Just remember that your product is more than simply the goods or services you have to sell. Your product is your people—how they represent your company, how they interact with clients, how they view their own professional lives. You want the highest-quality product you can offer to give your customers the best value. Be sure you think about your employees in the same way by offering them a solid team of peers within the company and the right kind of incentives to keep them excited, active, and content. Together, you will take your company to new heights.

CHAPTER 12

BE A STUDENT OF YOUR INDUSTRY

We love to dream of the day when we will finally have "made it"—when there is nothing left to do, nothing left to worry about, nothing left to learn. Unfortunately, for an entrepreneur, that day will never come.

Too many people fall into the trap of believing that once they reach a certain point, they can just maintain what they've built. That's the most surefire way to become obsolete.

No matter how successful your business, how long your client list, or how substantial your bank account, you always have to stay on top of the latest innovations in your industry. As long as you're part of the company, you have to be an eternal student.

Think about the world's most elite athletes. When Tiger Woods announced that he was going to redo his swing from the ground up because he had been studying and saw a way to improve what he was doing, people were shocked. Why would the world's best player relearn the game? It's simple: he wanted to *remain* the world's best player, so he did whatever he could to take his game to the next level.

A doctor must always stay abreast of the latest medical advancements and discoveries to best meet the needs of each patient. In the same way, experienced salespersons may have a detailed process that they use, but they constantly rework and refine the technique with each client they encounter.

They never let their approach go static, and they are always in tune with market trends and projections.

If you want to be a professional at anything, you have to study your field—not just as you prepare to enter it, but as you prepare to face it every day and into the future. The masters of anything, the best of the best, are constantly working at their game, practicing, studying, meeting with mentors, and even hiring coaches. It doesn't matter what field you're in; from basketball to business, this kind of dedication to your craft is the mark of a true professional.

My first suggestion is to stay in practice. Never allow yourself to get too far away from the nuts and bolts of your product and your sales plan. Stay involved with your accounts and selling techniques. Interact with customers. Even as your role may change from being the front man to managing your company behind the scenes, you should always keep a toe in the everyday business that makes your operation work.

But you want to do more than just stay in touch with the way things are run; you want to make sure that you stay informed and on the cutting edge of which way your industry is headed. And to do that, you are going to have to make a continual and deliberate effort to stay informed. Subscribe to trade magazines. Read blogs. Attend conferences in your field. You can even enroll in classes at the local community college or university to help you gain new certifications or keep abreast of new techniques.

 **Part of being a student of your industry is learning how to make connections and understanding their worth. Attend local business leader gatherings. Identify the ones that are a match for you, and take advantage of the opportunities they offer to meet, mingle, and learn.**

You can also reach out to people in a face-to-face effort, which can be one of the most effective means of staying informed.

We've talked about mentors and their importance in helping you construct your business plan and find your way in the industry when you're first getting started, but they definitely come into play at this stage of the game as well. Only now, they aren't teaching you the ropes so much as they are helping you refine what has already proven successful for your business.

One of the things to remember is that when you are the CEO of a business, you have no one to complain to. You can't show weakness or uncertainty. When people come to your company, they are doing so for security and confidence, and it is your responsibility to provide that to both your employees and clients alike.

With your clients, that's self-explanatory—they need to trust your product and your people. With your employees, your job is to get everybody focused on the company's vision and on winning, and you need to have a clear sense of how each employee contributes to that end. That means you need to be the expert in the room. The way to achieve that status is by being a student through your own study and research and by relying on a business coach/mentor to be your sounding board for ideas and opinions, and even for fears and uncertainties. You never want to lie to your employees about the way business is going, but it can be tremendously helpful to have a fellow professional who can listen to your concerns in private and offer sound advice so you can present confidence when you greet your employees to discuss the newest strategies, marketing plans, and product offerings of your company.

But how do you find the right person to be that confidant and mentor, now that you have several successful years under your belt and aren't just a new entrepreneur looking for direction?

Generally speaking, you have to network to find a good mentor. Hopefully, this is something that will have already come naturally to you as your business and client list have grown. Part of being a student of your industry is learning how to make connections and understanding their worth. Attend local business leader gatherings. Many communities offer a variety of networking opportunities, such as "Young Professionals" mixers or "Women in Business" conferences. Identify the ones that are a match for you, and take advantage of the opportunities they offer to meet, mingle, and learn.

I know from personal experience because I speak at many of these events. I have had individuals approach me afterward and say things like, "Ryan, here's my card with my contact information. What you said was extremely relevant to my business. I'm a student of the industry just like you, and my goal is to learn everything I possibly can about this industry because I want to build a very successful company within it. Do you mind if I take two or three minutes of your time to learn a few things from you?" My answer is always that I'd be happy to give that person a few minutes of my time because it is clear to me that such a person will have targeted, specific questions. If I see that you have confidence in your business and are looking to grow it beyond its current parameters, it tends to be a much easier mentoring job than talking through the intricacies of starting up a business with someone who is just launching his or her plan.

Additionally, if you hear a presentation given by a business leader you admire and by whom you hope to be coached or mentored, you can send him a note letting him know you heard his talk at that specific event and you would love the opportunity to meet with him further to gain his insight into your business and its current path. Personal introductions aren't always necessary; sometimes just a specific—if impersonal—encounter, such as being in the audience at a speech, can be a great first step in opening mentorship doors. I have been on both sides of this kind of letter, and the more specific you are with the points you raise about the speech or philosophies, the more likely you are to get a response.

The key to capturing the attention of a mentor you want to have as a business coach is, once again, to be a student of your industry. You must have researched the individual thoroughly—read every newspaper or magazine article printed about her, try to track down each TV or radio interview she's done, and learn whatever you can about her company. Only by doing your homework will you be in a position to ask the right kinds of questions that will set you apart from the other business owners seeking mentorship. Remember that Golden Rule: never ask a question you already know the answer to.

Consider, for a moment, what would happen if Michael Jordan were to sit down for an interview with a sports journalist who said, "Oh my gosh, you're just the best! Can you teach me how to be a successful basketball player?" He'd probably just smile and give some generic answer like, "Thanks. The secret to success is to work hard and never give up on your dreams." But if that same journalist were to say, "I've studied your game, and I notice that in certain circumstances, you tend to prefer X technique, which goes against conventional wisdom. Clearly it worked for you, though—would you mind explaining why you chose to play that way?" Suddenly, the reporter has Jordan's attention because he is demonstrating his own level of proficiency in the game as well as exhibiting specific knowledge of the person from whom he is seeking guidance.

Specific questions are much more likely to lead to specific answers, but to ask those kinds of questions, you have to be fully knowledgeable about the subject area and the person you're addressing. And to do that, you have to be a student of your industry.

The other thing to consider is how many potential mentors are out there who can speak to your specific issues. For example, if you run a bakery, how many high-end cake decorators do you know of who have created the kind of business you'd like yours to be?

It's simple. If there are 100 companies that have done what you want to do at the level you want to do it, then there are probably at least ten people who were a part of each of those hundred companies—not necessarily the CEO or the name on the sign, but key players in growing that business—who could give you mentorship in how to expand your company from where you are to where you want to be. That means you have a thousand people on the planet from whom you can draw. So how do you find those people?

First of all, many of those people may still be active in the industry. Is there a trade association? Is there some form of an annual conference? Is there an industry publication where these people will pen articles? Do any of them write blogs? Are they on Facebook, Twitter, or other social networks? Is there a place where these people, these experts, these authorities on the subject congregate—either locally, nationally, or through correspondence? Generally speaking, experienced mentors are all around us in one form or another, but we hardly ever notice them.

If you aren't in an environment that offers these kinds of opportunities, then you need to change your environment. You may need to drive a little farther to attend mixers and conferences, but remember that it is an investment in the future of your company. You simply have to be proactive with the objective to identify people from whom you can learn and with whom you can meet and work. Remember, you are a successfully business owner now. These are your peers, though perhaps with a little more experience or different insights. You deserve to be there, mingling with them confidently.

Another great way to make connections is through charity work. Just about every major business is involved in some kind of charity work. A great way to make connections with the kinds of mentors you want to find is by researching which companies work with which charitable organizations, and then plug in.

Any responsible, ethical business owner is going to be involved with something that gives back, whether it be at the community level, in combat against a specific disease, or in a broad campaign to address a specific concern. If you are willing to take the time to roll up your sleeves—first, to find out what groups your targeted mentor works with, and second, to start giving of your money, time, or resources with that same group—you can find inroads to business mentors very quickly, and all while pursuing a worthy cause.

But here's the thing: Not everyone is going to say yes. Not every potential mentor is going to respond positively to your introduction or answer your letter. And when that is the case, move on to the next 999 people who are relevant to your company. Once you look into it, you'll find that there really is a long list of people from whom you could draw some form of mentorship until you find the right match of relevant experience and knowledge, and the right chemistry between you and that person. You might very well hit it off with the person and have rapport and identification with each other, realizing, "Wow! We know some of the same people!" or, "We went to the same college," or, "That's great—we have the same views and values." You know you've hit the jackpot when the mentor you seek says, "You remind me of myself when I was at that stage in my career." I'll never forget when Russ Bik, a founder of Sun Microsystems, said that to me. When you make those kinds of connections, that's when you have your coach. That's when you have an open invitation to take the next step of asking for business mentorship.

But at this stage in the game, mentorship is more than just asking for advice—it's forming a kind of partnership. Now that you are in a position to do so, you should consider offering some form of compensation to your mentor, especially if he or she is acting in a business coach capacity or as an advisory board member.

For example, you could offer your coach a place on your board of directors or board of advisors. *Author's note: We've made it easy for you to set up your own board of advisors with the* Nothing to Lose *Facebook app. Install the app and get started now at apps.facebook.com/nothingtolose.* I have made this kind of offer before with my own businesses. I would invite the individuals whose expertise and advice I admired—and whose discretion I trusted—to serve on the board in exchange for equity in the company. Equity is the greatest currency that a company has. Be careful about giving out too much, but you definitely want to take advantage of what you've built to bring on board the right people to share your vision and help guide you in your continual quest to convert your knowledge of your field into a stronger company.

 **It is not the most uplifting perspective, but part of you should always be thinking about your business as headed down the road to extinction. You have to look for what's broken and what's not working—and bring in your trusted business coach or advisors to do the same thing.**

If you have a mentor, are seeking a specific a mentor, or have connected with a world-class business mind or a retired person from your industry who is willing to come in and help you, then give him or her a piece of the pie. Good mentors tend to take equity rather than cash in exchange for their time, and good CEOs understand the very valuable service that such an individual can provide to the company. I've negotiated deals that are part cash/part equity, and deals that are 100 percent either way. I've found that a combination of both seems to work best. It offers mentors an immediate value for their time, while also engaging them with the company.

Another way to gain insight as to the direction and growth of your industry is (to quote Sun Tzu again) to "know thy enemy." Interview your competition. Find out what is working and not working for them, who their vendors are, what their long-term plans are, and what connections they are making.

There are two ways to go about doing this. One is to find people who have recently left the other business and meet with them to learn whatever you can to make you more competitive. The other option is to identify what company you admire and want to emulate, and then try to hire qualified workers directly from them.

For example, when we were growing ViSalus, we knew we wanted to hire the former head of marketing at our biggest competitor. We had researched the field and learned that she was the topnotch professional out there for what we wanted, and we knew she had built up a great team. So we began by expanding our marketing department and listing the open jobs in such a way that members of her group would be specifically targeted. Sure enough, we made a number of hires as people left that company to join ours. As more people came, they brought with them new sets of skills, knowledge, and connections. We were able to learn about our competition's corporate structure and what was working for them, and as those employees shared the organizational plan and explained who the key players were, we were able to lure away some of the high-level executives up to the very top of the marketing department.

Obviously, you have to operate ethically if you choose to go this route—follow to the letter all nondisclosure contracts and noncompete clauses by which your new or potential employees may be legally bound. Additionally, you should never pressure people to give you information that they may feel is confidential or simply not right to share. But the talent wars are a very common practice in business, as well-informed employers seek out the rising stars in their field. If you have not kept yourself schooled in knowing who is making a name for themselves, what companies are growing, and what sectors hold the most promise, you may find yourself as the victim—rather than beneficiary—of just such a brain drain.

Perhaps the best way to bring this all into perspective is to think of your business as an old guitar that needs to be retuned each time you pick it up to play. Sometimes it's one thing, sometimes it's something else. The point is that each adjustment, no matter how major or minor, is going to affect the overall quality of the sound. Sometimes you get the knob set just right, and you might have a year or six months during which you don't even have to adjust anything. Sometimes you have to make a small tweak each time you pick it up. The market around you is always adjusting, and you have to be willing to adjust along with it.

Advancements in technology, especially, make things obsolete at a mind-boggling pace. Today, the aging process of the business is magnified probably a hundred times, compared with what it was twenty, thirty, or forty years ago. Obsolescence and even extinction occurs to Fortune 500 companies at a rate right now that's unlike anything that we've ever experienced before.

It used to be a simple pattern: if you joined a company, you were set for life—you worked there for thirty years, earned your gold watch, and then retired on its benefit plan. Things aren't quite that simple anymore. Because of technology, communication, knowledge, efficiency, and the global economy, the rate of extinction for certain industries and models is far greater than it ever has been, and a simple error of misjudging or ignoring a trend can create a major failure.

The biggest mistakes I've ever made in the history of my career have been when I haven't paid attention to the details or when I haven't thought through every single, little process that has potential for impact. That doesn't mean you should micromanage your people or your process, but if you're not thinking through the details, your employees probably aren't, either. If you really invest yourself in the study of your industry, the significance of certain details will begin to emerge as the most pressing. And it is these to which you will want to turn your focus, ask for advice, and seek improvement.

It is not the most uplifting perspective, but part of you should always be thinking about your business as headed down the road to extinction. You have to look for what's broken and what's not working—and bring in your trusted business coach or advisors to do the same thing with a fresh pair of eyes to help your business evolve.

The smallest crack in the foundation of a building can lead to an absolute collapse. You want to inspect your business as you would your home. In fact, there is an old management saying: "Inspect what you expect." If you expect profits, inspect how you generate them and how you create them. If you expect management to be detailed, inspect their priority lists.

I once heard a story about Henry Kissinger that recounted how he used to have his directors write up reports on their areas. A few days after he received them, he would call the manager into his office and say, "I don't believe this report reflects your best effort. I would like you to rewrite it." In reality, he had never read their reports at all; he was just always getting people to reach higher and to dig deeper. Kissinger's approach may not be the best for your business, but the goal of continually seeking improvement is one from which any company can profit.

A mentor I've studied for nearly a decade, Bob Goergen, taught me that there is no finish line in business. You must always be a willing student, ready to learn whatever is necessary to pass the next test. As long as you are a part of the company, you must continually be seeking out the information, people, and resources that will better equip you for the next week, the next year, and the next decade.

If you want to build something that will last, you need to be willing to outfit your company and yourself with the skills, tools, understanding, and foresight that will allow you to traverse the swells and currents of the market and the industry. It's not about the day when you've "made it" so you can finally relax—it's about working continually with an eye toward making it to each new day.

CHAPTER 13

IDENTIFY YOUR PRIORITIES

While it is obvious that it is essential to be a student of your industry, it is not always as obvious where the starting point for that study should be. Especially if you are in a large and varied industry such as technology, it can seem impossible and a little overwhelming to know just where you should focus your time and resources when researching upcoming trends and breaking developments.

It is essential to prioritize if you want to keep your business on solid footing both in the present and with whatever the future market may throw your way. As important as it is to fine-tune your business, you do not want to begin changing things at random. You will need to have a methodical and logical system that addresses the issues of the most importance (in other words, with the greatest potential impact, both positive and negative), and then continues to each subsequent matter in turn.

But just as it can be difficult to determine where to concentrate your priorities for growth and development, it can be equally overwhelming to try to prioritize the current day-to-day matters within your company's operations without even worrying about what might be coming down the pike in a year.

President Franklin D. Roosevelt once famously quipped, "The urgent problems are seldom the important ones." Indeed, the distinction between the urgent and the important is the key in maintaining a balanced view of your company's concerns. Urgent matters are those that have to be addressed right away because they are time-sensitive matters. Important issues are ones that have significant implications on your operations, products, services, or profit margin. But when both seem to be vying for your time, how do you determine which gets your attention first?

There is an old managerial trick that is probably the most reliable one I have encountered. I found it while reading Stephen Covey's book *Seven Habits of Highly Effective People.* Draw a square and draw a "t" down the middle, dividing it into four quadrants. Label one box "Urgent," one "Important," one "Urgent and Important," and the last "Neither Urgent nor Important." Armed with that visual aid, you can easily see how the intersection of urgency and importance is the most pressing quadrant that will need to be the first to garner your attention.

 **The key is to be intimately involved with your business to the point that you understand its intricacies well enough to know what needs to happen immediately and what can wait, and to be detached enough to view the situation with an unbiased eye so your decisions are not clouded by emotion.**

Each potential problem you encounter or issue that is raised, each improvement you would like to implement, and each change you feel is necessary will fall into one of those four categories. Your job is to figure out which one and then to respond accordingly. For example, if you have to get your design specs to the printer before the shop closes for the day, that's urgent. If you need to hire someone to fill a vacant sales post, that is important. If you have discovered that a batch of herb-roasted chicken your catering business just shipped to a wedding reception may have been contaminated with E. coli, that's urgent *and* important. Each matter is clamoring for your time—which should get your attention first?

Obviously, in this case the answer is clear—you have to intercept the van carrying the contaminated food, make sure no one consumes it, decontaminate your kitchen and equipment, make sure that there has been no cross-contamination with other foods you've prepared, and come up with an alternative serving plan so that the guests won't be left with empty plates. That's a lot to manage all at once, but it certainly makes getting those new designs to the printer seem a little less pressing, doesn't it?

The same principle applies when it comes to prioritizing your industry research. There are urgent issues: what new promotion is your local competition planning to launch next week, and how can you act in an equally customer-attracting way? There are important issues: new government regulations that could have an impact on your operations are under debate and may go into effect in the next year. And there are the issues that are both urgent and important: a study was just released that shows customers flocking to a new type of product that outperforms yours in price, capability, and customer satisfaction.

You need to dedicate time to researching each one of these issues, but you have to be able to figure out which issue to attack first so you can maximize both your time and effectiveness in understanding and responding to each one.

Some scenarios, such as the catering one above, are obvious. Others aren't quite so clear-cut. When you're thinking about your business—something you have painstakingly designed, grown, and fostered through your own blood, sweat, and tears—everything seems to be both urgent and important, from the colors you choose for your new business cards (Do they look professional and convey the right image? Do they help to create brand recognition?) to how quickly shipments make it out the door (Are we meeting our deadlines? Do we have adequate supply to fulfill each order?).

The key is to be intimately involved with your business to the point that you understand its intricacies well enough to know what needs to happen immediately and what can wait, and to be detached enough to view the situation with an unbiased eye so your decisions are not clouded by emotion. It's a tough balance to find, but it is a necessary one to maintain.

One extremely helpful way of making these kinds of judgments is to involve your management team and their evaluations. If they are able to distinguish between what is urgent and what is important, they will be able to advise you in your executive decisions and can help put out fires in their own departments without any matters but the most serious even having to cross your desk. Sometimes your management can see the forest through the trees when you can't.

Your managers can also help with prioritizing by investing themselves in industry research. Many companies will cover the cost or even guarantee increased compensation for continuing studies in relevant fields. It is also common to require employees in certain fields to attend at least one trade seminar each year for the sake of hearing new pitches, spotting emerging products, and networking with different groups of people. Any kind of effort such as this will help strengthen your company not only through broadening perspectives and skill sets, but also by helping each level of the corporate structure grasp the company's priorities and implement them in their own management and operations.

But how do you motivate your managers and employees alike to prioritize the things that will keep your business growing and prospering? It's the same idea that was so important when we discussed hiring them in the first place. It's one of my Golden Rules, and it's a simple truth: compensation drives behavior.

If an employee discovers a bottleneck in the production process and brings that to his or her manager's attention, that deserves recognition. If a manager looks at your facilities and realizes a more cost-efficient way to organize things and suggests it to you, celebrate that. In short, anytime someone in the company takes the initiative to look around with an eye toward improvement, that is worth noting and rewarding. The reward could take any form, from a small salary increase to a one-time bonus to a special award. It could even be something as small as a gift card to a local restaurant. The point is that you should do *something* to motivate and honor behavior that aligns with the priorities of your company.

Your employees spend your money and make your money, so make sure they prioritize saving and making money. I know it sounds simple, but all too often we assume as entrepreneurs that our employees treat our money as though it was their own. Sometimes, however, they don't, because occasionally, saving money and making money can come at the expense or comfort of the employee. At SkyPipeline, one of my employees made an error with an account, and we lost a customer as a result. I took that employee aside and explained the lifetime value of that customer and how a careless error had cost us over $100,000 in the long run. The employee had no idea that a $1,000-per-month account was worth $100,000 to the company. Needless, to say he didn't make any more $100,000 errors. Your job as the CEO is to insist that the highest priority is for each employee to either save you money, make you money, or both.

The more your employees see that prioritizing is valued, the more they will become engaged in the behavior as well. Soon, your company will have a culture of excellence that permeates every level, and your company will be healthier, thanks to the constant attention and concern of everyone involved.

It is also possible to turn prioritizing into a kind of friendly competition between departments. Just as compensation can be a great motivator in increasing sales and efficiency plans in each department, you can also give special recognition to entire departments that step up at crucial times and manage their priorities in the most effective way. Even if it's simply that they get to go through the serving line first at the company picnic, some kind of genuine thanks can go a long way in reinforcing the value you place on their attentiveness. This not only encourages a sense of camaraderie among the members of that particular team, but it also reminds your other departments of the important place that prioritizing holds within your company's structure.

You will want to make sure that the right kind of prioritizing is being encouraged, though. Make sure your employees understand the difference between the important and the urgent. Deadlines are both urgent and important, but quality is even more so. If someone spots a flaw in an order and immediately brings it to the attention of his or her superiors, that action should be praised. It takes courage to point out errors. An employee who is willing to stick out his or her neck for the sake of doing the right thing and protecting the company in turn is the kind of employee you want to keep around and the kind of vigilance you want to foster among all of your workers.

The issue of quality raises another issue to think about in terms of prioritizing, and that is how well you know your market's needs.

When I first took over SkyPipeline, I was faced with the difficult decision of how to grow the business. I knew we needed to expand both in terms of what we offered and in the areas where we made our services available. The challenge was that I really only had the resources at first to grow in one direction, not both.

I finally decided that if we were able to offer a superior product in the area where we were already operating, that would be a smarter move for the company than offering unreliable service to a broader range of people. To reference the quote from *Art of War* in my Golden Rules, "An army everywhere is an army nowhere."

In the end, it would be a more effective use of our resources to concentrate on smaller growth with larger offerings than to be constantly making service calls and fielding complaints from a much larger geographical region while we developed a better product.

What resulted from that decision ended up being the key to our success. Because we prioritized quality over market expansion, we were able to attract larger accounts, which also brought us bigger investors because we consistently offered top-notch service to our limited area. As our reputation grew, so did the demand for our product. And with that growth, we were able to secure the capital we needed to expand our business to meet the needs of customers in a much larger area by offering them the same quality product we had developed as our top priority.

The secret is to know your company and to know your client base. The prioritizing I did with SkyPipeline is not always the right choice. We were originally serving mostly a wealthy clientele who were willing to pay more for a better product and who, because of their professional obligations, placed a premium on having confidence in the reliability of our services.

In other cases, however, there may not be as much of a demand for the bells and whistles. Some markets are better suited for basic offerings that meet a need at a minimal cost. Consider, for example, the cell phone market. While some companies are constantly releasing more sophisticated phones with capabilities ranging from cameras to music downloads to Internet access, other companies are capitalizing on the other end of the market for people who don't want any of the accessories—just a basic device for making calls. Some of these are even marketed specifically to the elderly, who may find the extra functions confusing, or to parents of small children, who just want a phone with three preprogrammed numbers to call in case of an emergency.

The point is, there is a market for both types of products, but companies must have a clear sense of priority in how they develop their products so they are meeting the right needs in the right way.

But prioritizing is not just limited to your company's output. You need to have your own set of private priorities that dictate how you interact with your company's day-to-day operations and how you function as an administrator. For example, is it more important to you to be hands-on so you know things are being done the right way, or do you think it is more important to back off and to function more in a consulting role? Both practices are probably going to be necessary, but you need to determine which is more important to you in terms of your primary approach.

You are going to need to develop a clear sense of how you divide your time and your attention so your executive point of view is dedicated first and foremost to the most valuable matters. By modeling effective prioritizing in your own life, you are also demonstrating to your managers how you expect them to set the priorities within their own sphere of influence, maximizing your most valuable resources—time and insight.

 **Make your decisions and carry them out with confidence. If you have kept yourself invested in your industry by being a student of it, and if you stay plugged into your company by studying it, the right place for your focus will probably make itself apparent.**

The same is also true with regard to business ethics. Of all of the principles at work in your business, what are the ones that you feel are the most important, the ones that you feel must rise to the top of the heap, the ones that trump all the other important beliefs? These values are the ones that you need to give the most time and attention to, from making sure that they are front and center in the workplace and strongly instilled in every employee to practicing them daily in your own behavior to ensure that you have made them a priority in your own life, as well.

Of course all of our business ethics are important, but by focusing extra attention on the most fundamental and unshakable ones that you hold dear, you can set the tone for how the rest are to be carried out without exhaustively reminding everyone in your company like a nagging parent or lecturing teacher.

Consider the current bank crisis. The leaders of so many corporations prioritized making an easy profit over doing the right thing, and it not only brought down their companies, but it also sent the nation's economy into a freefall that has affected just about every industry and job market. The misplaced priorities of a few leaders corrupted the culture of their entire business so the company was no longer sustainable.

Establishing and maintaining your personal and company-wide priorities will help keep your business on track, provided your priorities are rooted in the right philosophies. Meet the needs of your market in an effective, sustainable, and responsible manner. While you should continually be on the lookout for new opportunities or better approaches, you should never allow the allure of profit to reshuffle the priorities you have established and the principles by which you established them.

As you navigate the sometimes-tricky world of identifying and then acting upon your priorities, you will likely begin to find that patterns emerge. With each determination of *urgent* versus *important*, you will start to find that the decisions become more natural, more innate. With each suggestion presented by an employee, you will start to see a developing sense of ownership and pride emerge among your workforce, as they feel themselves further invested in the overall operations and output of the company.

As potentially overwhelming as the matter may first appear, the more you identify and then follow through with your decision on what to act upon and how to address it, the easier subsequent determinations will become. Make your decisions and carry them out with confidence. If you have kept yourself invested in your industry by being a student of it, and if you stay plugged into your company by studying it, the right place for your focus will probably make itself apparent.

At the same time, you should never adhere blindly to your priorities. Remember the old saying, "Sometimes the fastest way forward is by going backward." If you find that you have made a mistake in prioritizing, don't be afraid to correct it rather than continuing down the wrong path in pursuit of the wrong thing. You have obviously made enough right choices and determined the right priorities along the way to land you where you are. Trust your entrepreneurial instinct, even as you hone and develop it.

Don't lose sight of the principles by which you created the company, and don't let the details of running it tear your focus from the big picture. Just keep a keen and distinguishing eye on the direction you hope to pursue, and with each step, make sure that your goals and ideals are following in line.

CHAPTER 14

DO I STAY OR GO?

There will come a point in your company's life when you are faced with a tough decision: should you stay on with the business you've built, or is it time to move on, either to new opportunities or to a different role in your business?

It is a serious and deeply personal decision that no one else can make for you. In this chapter, I want to lay out the various scenarios and possibilities to consider when you do find yourself faced with this choice, and I will suggest things you should consider if you find yourself inclined toward making an exit.

Phil Jackson, coach of the Los Angeles Lakers, loved to say, "Every life has a cycle, and too many people stay on longer than they should, and they actually reduce the value of what it is they've accomplished." Now that you have gone from being unemployed, unhappy in your job, or just starting to build your dreams to actually having a successful product, company, and business structure, how do you know when the time is right for you to finish your game and celebrate what you've accomplished—and how do you exit the court gracefully?

As you begin considering the future, you will need to evaluate the various options open to you. The three most important are timing (Is this the best time for me to leave the company?), direction (In what direction do I see both my company and the industry headed?), and opportunity (What options are out there right now that are worth more examination as potential means for an exit?).

Timing can be both a subjective issue and an objective one. In the first case, there are any number of factors you may find weighing on your mind: your health and energy, other dreams you want to pursue, family issues, a desire to retire to another part of the country—any one of these could affect how you view the issue.

If you are an individual who thrives on the dynamics of business and the competition of the marketplace, you may feel that it is time to exit when the thrill of the entrepreneurial spirit is gone from your company. If you feel you have maximized the potential of your management team because you have a comfortable and solid market share, you may be interested in selling to pursue other business ventures. Maybe you want to explore a different industry, or you find yourself intrigued by new ideas. Green Business, for example, is highly valuable right now, and perhaps you are interested in trying your hand at developing a technology that reduces carbon footprints while the timing is right for such a pursuit. Whatever the case, this kind of restlessness is very common among entrepreneurs because of the innate competitive nature that drives many of us to this field in the first place. My venture capitalist friends call this Founder's Syndrome—when it's time for the founder(s) to move on, either by one's own desire or by that of a board member or investor.

 **If you do determine that the time is right for you to leave, you can't simply walk out the door one day and be done with it. You need to have an exit strategy that sets your business up for a smooth transition and a successful future. If nothing else, you owe that to your stakeholders.**

On the other hand, there may be other forces at work that determine whether the timing is right or less than ideal. For example, a person looking to sell his home construction business in Southern California would have made a killing if he had sold it in 2007. If you know that the market is at a high in your field, that might affect your decision. Conversely, that same individual would have a much more difficult time selling his business in 2009, simply because of the downturn in the market. If your industry is currently in a slump, that can also alter your perspective on whether now is the right time to leave.

This also points to the next factor you need to consider: direction. Are you in tune with the markets? Do you have a sense of which way the trends are starting to point? Once again, this is why being a student of your industry is so crucial—you have to have your finger on the pulse of the market to know the wisest move for the future of your company.

For example, after several years of growing and developing SkyPipeline, it became clear to me that cell phone companies were going to give us a run for our money. I didn't want to be in the business of trying to fight that, and neither did my investors. I know that there are some people who relish that kind of challenge, but for me, I felt that I wanted to explore other options to go along with the new direction of the industry rather than carve out a niche contrary to it. Because I was able to see where our field was headed and project what kinds of issues we would be facing, I knew that I was not in a business I wanted to stay in, so I began looking for buyers who *were* interested in that kind of business. We reached out to a few of our competitors and asked whether there was an interest in combining our businesses. Two emerged, and we successfully sold the company to the highest-bidding competitor.

Even if the industry itself is not headed in a direction you want to avoid, you may find that it is time for the company to take a new direction—and that you are not the person best suited to do that. Perhaps you no longer feel you can contribute as a founder the way you once did or that your research indicates that it is better for your company to diversify or specialize. Perhaps such a shift does not play to your strongest skills, but you have a brilliant person in mind who would be an ideal leader. It could be that now is the time to hand over control to a new CEO who can take what you've established and built and grow your company to new heights.

Finally, you will want to consider the various opportunities that are out there, or are likely to be out there in the next few years. If you have someone with a generous buyout offer right now, you may want to take a serious look at it to see if this particular opportunity is, in fact, your best option. Do you want to hand over the company to someone who cares about it, knows the business, and is willing to pay you a premium that will make the years you invested in it seem worth it?

You may also be looking ahead toward other opportunities that may be coming down the pike so you can prepare your company and be able to maximize the benefits. For example, if you recognize that Microsoft will probably begin trending toward a certain area over the next twenty-four to forty-eight months, and your company has an effective product in that market, you may want to begin to position your company to be appealing to Microsoft as they look to absorb smaller businesses that can meet that particular need. You stand to benefit from the company's sale, and your employees stand to benefit from job security and opportunities with a major corporation. Below, we will discuss how to begin aligning your company so you are poised for just such an offer.

If you do determine that the time is right for you to leave, you can't simply walk out the door one day and be done with it, though. You need to have an exit strategy that sets your business up for a smooth transition and a successful future. If nothing else, you owe that to your stakeholders.

The first way to exit is probably the most appealing to a majority of people, and that is to retire while maintaining an interest that continues to earn you money. It's commonly referred to as Golden Handcuffs—a play on the Golden Parachute idea for big-name CEOs leaving with huge severance packages. Whether you have a home-based business or twenty-five franchise locations, Golden Handcuffs are a permanent tie to your company that bring you residual profits while keeping you close enough to the business to give your advice, meet with shareholders, and to go over corporate affairs as the need arises.

In many cases this isn't an exit, but rather getting a good team to run the company under your supervision for the long-term. To some people, this isn't appealing—when they retire, they want it to be a clean separation. For other people, this is the perfect arrangement that allows them to enjoy the benefits of what they've created while also allowing them to stay active in the business they love. This is also a good system for maintaining the confidence of investors or shareholders, who are often spooked by a complete handover of power. By retaining a presence within the company, albeit a limited one, you can help ease fears of the unknown and still add value to the enterprise.

For this kind of exit to be successful, though, you have to make sure that you have left the books in order and that you appoint the right people to whom you will hand over the reins of leadership as you move toward a lesser role. We'll discuss more about that a little later.

The second way to exit is through a merger or acquisition. In other words, if there is an interested person or group who wishes to purchase the business from you at a fair price, it may be an offer worth considering. Likewise, if another company makes an offer to fold yours into its own operations, you may also have a good opportunity to leave, while knowing that your years of effort will carry on, and your employees will have continued stability. A merger or an acquisition can be a very complicated transaction. I've been on the buying side a few times, as well as on the selling side. SkyPipeline merged with NextWeb, which was bought by Covad Communications. Fusion merged with ViSalus and was bought by Blyth. PathConnect's technology went on to create a variety of new businesses spanning multiple industries. I have been a part of several merger and acquisition deals and, fingers crossed, might one day find myself on the buyer or seller side again.

Your final option is to take the company public so that shareholders—in addition to you—become the owners. In this scenario, rather than selling to one party, you are selling part of the company to anyone who wants to own a share, and you are allowing it to be traded on the stock exchange. In the interest of full disclosure, I should tell you that I have never taken a company public. At ViSalus, we were heavily considering taking our company public on the London Stock Exchange in late 2007. We had a term sheet from a billion-dollar hedge fund to help with that move, but after careful consideration, we decided to sell to Blyth. As a young CEO, I thought the idea of going public was exciting. I dreamed of billions in market capitalization and $100 stock; however, that wasn't the reality I was facing, and I must admit, I am glad I'm not running a public company in today's economy. In fact, we dodged a bullet by not doing that deal. Luckily, our company was generating a lot of cash, and we had all exit options on the table. We chose the partner and the transaction that, I believe, was best for our customers, distributors, and employees.

When I was leaving SkyPipeline, we first merged with another small company called NextWeb, then sold our combined equity to Covad, which was a public company. At the time I made my exit, the stock was trading at about $0.70 a share, and when I sold my shares, they were about $2.60 each. Many of my investors followed suit and made up to five or six times their initial investment because of our exit plan and strategy; others chose to remain invested in the company and saw the company go through some difficult times before it was eventually bought for $1.05 per share. Those investors didn't yield the same return as those of us who took our money off the table. My responsibility was to get them liquidity so they could determine how much money they wanted to make, and that was exactly what we did. It ended up being a good strategy for the business because I couldn't develop it the way it needed to be developed, but NextWeb/Covad had the means and the interest to do just that. My investors could then decide for themselves whether they wanted to align with the new company or move their interests elsewhere.

From a financial point of view, the Golden Handcuffs solution is almost always the most preferable because it leaves the greatest number of assets in your name, which translates to greater profits—not just during your lifetime, but as part of your estate. Mergers and acquisitions are never easy, with their legal wranglings and contract terms. They also can potentially endanger the jobs of some of your employees who may be let go because their positions duplicate those that already exist in the other company. This is called consolidated savings, and it is a common practice to buy a company with an eye toward consolidating. Also, a company's bid to go public may not be successful if it is not large enough and profitable enough to generate sufficient public interest in purchasing it. I know many public company CEOs who wish that they were with private companies because of the challenges that being a public company brings.

But each situation is different, and if a merger will open new markets for your product, it may end up being the wisest option. Or, if you feel that the investment potential of a publicly traded company is what your business needs to reach the next level, then these might be right choices for you after all. Again, this is a decision that, ultimately, only you will be able to make.

If you want to take the route of offering your company for sale, you will probably have a number of different options for marketing your company. There are business brokers and investment bankers who specialize in how to approach the marketplace to sell your business. You may also find yourself talking to local competitors, as we will discuss a little later on. Whatever the case, when you are involved in selling your company, the most important thing you can possibly do is hire a good lawyer to pore over the details and negotiate the best possible contract. In the ViSalus/Blyth transaction, we spent over a million dollars on attorneys to ensure that the right deal was reached for both parties.

When ViSalus merged with Blyth, the contract was ninety-six pages long and full of legalese. I remember spending hours on the phone reviewing every line of every page with all of the deal's team: our attorneys, our executive board, and our management team. We had people on the line from New York, Philadelphia, Miami, and Los Angeles, and we read over every single word of that contract. That is what we had to do, because it literally meant millions to each of us.

Unfortunately, many entrepreneurs make the mistake of thinking, "I hired the lawyer to write that contract for me; I'm not going to read every word of it." That's the biggest mistake that you can possibly make in an exit. During the ViSalus transaction, I was trying to push through the agreement when one of my advisors stopped me and, in an almost-yelling tone, said, "Ryan, we are going to read every single word, *every word*, on this call." There were ninety-six pages, 100 words a page, and six people on the call—it took over four hours. But that was an important lesson for which I am grateful, because I learned that you have to make sure you understand every bit and piece of the deal so you know where you stand, where your employees stand, and where your company stands after the deal is finalized. Don't be afraid to stop the meetings and ask questions. Sometimes the concepts are very complex, and only the pros in the room will fully grasp them. Make sure that you understand everything, and don't be intimidated to ask, "What does that mean to me, specifically?" In one deal, I stopped the meeting several times to ask questions, saying, "Pardon me, I am not familiar with this concept and how it applies to _____. Will you please explain it to me in detail?" Truth be told, sometimes I knew exactly what they were talking about, but I wanted to make sure everyone in the room understood it, too. Either way, it is your job to make sure you and your team fully understand everything to which you are agreeing.

 **You will never be able to replicate yourself perfectly, but you will want to choose someone with similar beliefs, philosophies, priorities, and principles, which is why a detailed understanding of how your company does business is so important.**

I want to insert a note here on the importance of making sure your employees are well taken care of after your exit. I made the mistake, after selling one of my companies, of not doing the homework and contract negotiations necessary to look after the very people who helped to make the company successful. I was focused on the exit and didn't understand that the new company was going to have a different approach than I did, including wanting to consolidate the operations. Suddenly, many very talented and loyal people who had been with me from the beginning found themselves out of work. It was heartbreaking to see them get the short end of the stick.

That was a very difficult situation to come to terms with when I realized what had happened—I had not looked ahead to what was awaiting them all when I turned over the operations. Keep your exit plan in view as you make those final decisions that will affect so many lives, and remember that your employees' welfare should always be part of your consideration.

As appealing as exit strategies can sound to entrepreneurs who are just starting out and who are facing the toughest phase of their business, it is essential to remember that (in my opinion) no business should be established with the sole aim of exiting. Your goal should be to create something that will allow you to leave it behind for generations to come. Exiting through cash flow should be every entrepreneur's dream. This means that your company is profitable and generates enough cash to pay its shareholders (in this case, you) a distribution of cash, sometimes referred to as a dividend. So, if your company was successful enough to generate $100,000 in profit every month after taxes, and you own 80 percent, you earn $80,000 per month—for the rest of your life! This is how successful companies develop, and companies that are not profitable or not focused on the long term do not attract interested investors or buyers—at least, not in this economy.

You should always be focused on building a successful, profitable business. Dream big, but focus on the small things. Building a successful business is going to bring you all the opportunities you need.

I highly recommend that you set up your business from the very first day with the idea that you are going to stay with it for the rest of your life. And before you consider leaving, ask yourself first if there is a way to reinvent yourself within the company.

When I was fund raising for ViSalus, I met with Brian McLoughlin, a venture capitalist from Global Retail Partners in Los Angeles. We were discussing what the term sheet would look like if Global Retail Partners decided to put money into ViSalus and buy some of our personal shares. During the conversation he asked me, "If you get all this money, what are you going to do next?"

I looked him in the eye and said, "I'm going to build ViSalus."

Brian smiled. That's the commitment every VC is looking for. He said, "Good, because the entrepreneurs who are the most successful are the ones that stick with their businesses." For example, the two founders of Google, Larry Page and Sergey Brin. They brought on Eric Schmidt, after a painstaking search for a CEO, and picked the right guy to replace them in the duties that they weren't right for. Eric helped take Google from less than $100 million to more than $100 billion. In short, Google got the right guy.

Now, if you have considered the alternatives, and still come to the conclusion that it is time to exit your company, it's essential that you make sure your business is in good financial order.

In one acquisition I was considering, I pulled out because the company I was seeking to buy was not in financial order. I lost confidence in the business and retracted my offer during due diligence. This cost both parties lots of money, but for me, it wasn't worth the potential liabilities. Now when I advise an entrepreneur setting up a company, I tell them to I follow all the requirements necessary to take it public eventually. Maybe one day they will take it public, or maybe one day a public company will want to buy their company. Either way, if your house is not in order, people will not want to buy it, especially not at a premium.

Hopefully, you have been keeping solid accounts of everything and have maintained good records of business matters, taxes, permits, etc. Unfortunately, not everyone does this. I have seen countless entrepreneurs who would like to sell their businesses, but they are completely unable to produce tax records or payroll information for a year or two prior, or they are unable to answer even basic questions about their accounting procedures. This is unacceptable. It does not position you well for continued prosperity after the handover, and it certainly does not make the business appealing to potential buyers, because there may be substantial liabilities that aren't disclosed. This lack of organization will cost you far more time and money down the road when a buyer pulls out or offers to buy you at a discounted value. You have to make sure that every single aspect of your business is ready to be audited. In fact, most professional investors will require audited financials.

 **Don't make the mistake of putting on an overly aggressive front when meeting with your competitors. You should be a strong representation of your company, but don't overdo it in the hopes of impressing or intimidating them.**

Believe me, I understand that when a company is first launched, the owner often does not have the time, knowledge, or understanding of some of these areas to be able to keep solid records on them all. I know I didn't at first, and that's understandable—it can be incredibly overwhelming. But at some point, that has to change. If loose management becomes the established pattern for the company, any buyer is going to be leery of what else has been misman-aged—and what the potential repercussions or liabilities of such laziness might be. At some point, a business has to become financially disciplined to be sustainable into the future and certainly for the owner to have a successful exit. The most important hire for most entrepreneurs is their CFO, because the CFO's role is to enforce financial discipline and make sure the business model is being followed. This is one of the most important—and expensive—lessons I have learned in my career: hire a great CFO!

The next thing to consider is who will be taking over for you. This is espe-cially important if you plan to maintain ownership of the company, because your ability to retire will depend on that person's ability to keep the business profitable. But even if you are not sticking around, you will still want to make sure that the right people are in certain key positions when you leave so the transition to new ownership is smooth and as positive as possible for the company you created. After all, one of the proudest reflections you will have is the success of your company long after you have left it.

You will want to make sure that you choose someone who is intimately famil-iar with your business. This usually means hiring from inside the company, though not always. This is usually why in family businesses, the retiring parent will hand over control to a child. The reason isn't just nepotism—that they want Junior to have the high-paying job behind the mahogany desk. In many cases, the children have grown up around the company. It's been a part of their lives since they were small. They've watched the operations for decades, they know the employees by name, and they've heard business discussions around the dinner table since elementary school. That kind of deeply ingrained knowledge and understanding also leads to a sense of loyalty to the business. No one wants to be the person who undoes Mom's life work or runs Grandpa's company into the ground.

But sometimes family isn't the best choice. Maybe the child pursued a different career path or the parent feels the leadership and maturity required for the job isn't there. Maybe there is simply a more qualified person waiting in the wings. Whatever the situation, when you choose your successor, you need to be able to make the decision that you feel is best for the future of the company.

Don't let emotion or feelings of obligation crowd your thinking. You want to make sure that whomever you choose truly "gets" not only the product and marketplace of your business, but also the culture of your company. You will never be able to replicate yourself perfectly, but you will want to choose someone with similar beliefs, philosophies, priorities, and principles, which is why a detailed understanding of how your company does business is so important.

Large corporations often hire new CEOs from other companies, but usually from the same industry. And when an outsider is brought in, he or she is surrounded by an executive board and management team who can offer the specific experience within the company that the new CEO is lacking. What this newcomer has to offer, though, will always be something fresh, either a new perspective or a different management style—something that the company needs to grow in a positive direction. But again, when someone new is brought in from outside the company to assume the helm, the CEO's offerings are always supplemented by the insider knowledge from others. He or she must thoroughly understand your company.

If you are seeking to sell your business, you will want to keep a similar mindset. Talk to investment bankers about which corporations are buying and selling in your industry, and approach local competitors or even national players that may be open, too. Very often, both the independent businesses and franchises in your area will be interested in folding successful local businesses—and their clientele—into their companies. That way, you know you are handing over control to someone who understands the industry and the craft. Doctor and veterinarian offices often follow the model of passing on the torch as one retires and a new person steps in. There is often a period where the new owner shadows the exiting one to meet patients, learn cases, and get a feel for the daily operations.

This same model can be very effective in any kind of business, since it gives your clients continuity and the comfort of seeing that you have personally selected who is taking over. If you are selling to someone directly, you can often negotiate retaining a small piece of ownership, as well. But as with picking a successor to a business you still own completely, you have to choose someone you trust as a person and a professional, and someone with whom you have a history. I recommend detailed background checks on prospective partners or buyers, just to make sure there aren't any unpleasant surprises lurking.

Even if you're planning to sell off the business completely, it is imperative to create an exit plan that sets your business up for success. Start engaging with prospective strategic partners early on. Use some of their services in your own company, and reach out to them with partnership ideas; this builds relationships and trust. It also enables you to learn how the other company works and lets you understand the entire landscape of the industry in a better way. SkyPipeline had a working relationship with NextWeb before we merged, which was helpful because even as competitors, we had a mutual respect for one another. They admired our sales and marketing, and we admired their operational capacities. When we joined forces a year later, the transition was much smoother because that relationship was already in place.

Try to make competitive relationships amiable; don't make the mistake of putting on an overly aggressive front when meeting with your competitors. You should be a strong representation of your company, but don't overdo it in the hopes of impressing or intimidating them. I did that very thing in a meeting once, and it drove my small local competitor into the arms of a much bigger competitor. Their resulting merger hurt us a great deal. I will never forget the dinner I had with the owner of my number-one competitor at SkyPipeline. He was open to a merger, and I jumped right to how I was going to launch a marketing campaign to go after every one of his customers if he didn't do a deal with me. At the end of the meeting, our COO, Mark Ozur, pulled me aside and said, "I can't believe you. You need to learn how to build rapport and not be so competitive." He was right. Instead of the way I acted, I suggest you keep things civil, and even pleasant, so that when the time comes for you to buy them, or for them to buy you, you've already built a bridge to a possible transaction.

I should point out, though, that the exit scenario is not always a rosy one. Remember that you are still largely beholden to your investors and their expectations. I know of entrepreneurs who have had their investors' money tied up for eight or nine years without any returns, which obviously leaves the investors less than happy. In situations like this, the CEO is sometimes given the ultimatum to get returns quickly or to step down and make way for someone who can.

If you are in the position in which you have not yet made good on your investment promises, you should not consider leaving until you have or until your board forces you out. It all goes back to some of those most fundamental lessons in business: you must be a good guardian of your investors' money, and you have to make sure that you're doing your best to satisfy the expectations that you set with them initially.

As you make the decision about exiting, look back over your career to consider what you've built and what kind of legacy you are leaving behind. Are you satisfied with all you have done in the company you've created? The jobs you've provided? The contribution you've made to your community? The charitable works to which you've contributed? What about the satisfied customers for whom you've provided a quality product or a needed service? How about changes you've brought to the industry or advancements you've helped champion? In short, can you evaluate your efforts, understanding that there will always be growing pains and a learning curve, and say with peace, "I did my best"?

Imagine the gratification of a CEO or a founder of a company like Phil Knight, seeing his Nike products on people's feet as they walk down the street. Most consumers couldn't pick Phil Knight out of a crowd or sitting at a restaurant—but people do know that they love his shoes. He created value in our society. He created something remarkable and greater than himself.

Warren Buffet remarked in an interview that he likes to buy companies that really contribute to society in some way. He likes to see the contribution. If he finds himself consuming the product, then he's looking at a good company to buy. That's an incredible level of satisfaction that only entrepreneurs can really appreciate when they see their product being consumed, enjoyed, and making a difference—long after they have stepped back from the helm.

Of course, for many entrepreneurs, the drive may be there to start all over again and try something else. Likewise, there may be a strong desire to stay connected to your company the way some people, like the aforementioned Google founders, have done; they are famous for still diving into the day-to-day business, even after accumulating billions of dollars, twelve years of experience, and being replaced as CEOs.

I've bought and sold three companies and I have no regrets because the experience taught me a very good lesson: if you don't have to start all over again—don't. When I left SkyPipeline I had to find a new team, test new marketing ideas, persuade new investors; it felt like starting from scratch without the family I was comfortable working with. Sure I had more money, but I realized that my true wealth wasn't in my bank account, it was in the team I had been cultivating and developing for years. As a result I swore I'd never lose a team like that again.

However you feel is fine—the question is simply whether you are proud of what you have been able to accomplish with your business. The sad truth is that some entrepreneurs never quite see the opportunity beyond where they are today. They turn their efforts into a glorified job, just like what they had before they left the corporate world to try things on their own. They have created their own Death Cycle in which they are forced to show up and deal with a management structure that is ineffective and unmotivated employees who are not right for the job. To me, this is about the most disappointing result of an entrepreneurial effort. Don't allow yourself to slip into that rut. Of course there will be difficult times and low periods for your business, but never lose sight of where you are headed. You want to be able to look back with satisfaction on all you have done.

When Blyth bought ViSalus, we made almost a dozen millionaires on the spot, and laid the foundation for many more to cross that threshold over the next several years. Just knowing that a company I helped to grow could so drastically change those lives was an incredible reward. That's always been one of my dreams—to build businesses that support families, create value, and make positive changes of some sort in people's lives. Sure, I occasionally dream about one day getting a call from Microsoft to tell me they want to give me a billion dollars for my business. That's in the back of my mind, but I don't build the business in such a way that the Microsoft scenario is my only measurement of success. I build companies with an eye toward contribution and marketplace revolution.

And that's the same reason you took this gamble in the first place—the reason you decided to risk it all and plunge into the world of business ownership. You knew there was something you wanted to accomplish, and you believed that you had the ability and tenacity to make it happen.

As you prepare to exit your company through whatever route you have determined is best, look back on what you have done with satisfaction, gratification, and pride. This company is your creation, an extension of your creativity, hard work, and dreams. And you accomplished it all because you understood the simple truth: you had nothing to lose.

EPILOGUE

A Great Time for America

I sometimes hear people say, "But if it takes me a year to get my business started and five years to really get it rolling and growing, I'll be ____ years old by the time I'm well established." My response to that is simple: how old will you be in a year or five years if you *don't* start your business?

Now is the time to resolve to do the thing you've always dreamed of doing. Now is the time to decide to act. Yes, money is tight right now, but the world of entrepreneurship has never been for the faint of heart—not even in the best of economic circumstances. As I stated at the opening of this book, if you can make it now, you can make it anytime.

If this is the step you want to take, there is no time like the present. If you are in the unemployment line right now, what would you give to get out of it and start working again—not just in any job, but in a field that you are passionate about? If you are caught in the Death Cycle, how soon do you want to be able to fire your boss and walk out of those doors to a new life, one in which you're in control? Or maybe you are thinking about starting up a business on the side, and you're looking forward to the day when you can tell you supervisor, "I don't have time for this job anymore because with my side business, I'm currently making more than you are."

But here is the thing to remember: no matter how great your idea or how revolutionary your product, no matter how talented you are as a salesman or a manager, you must have a supportive group of family or friends to encourage you through the rough patches, and you've got to have great employees who help you get the job done. Of course, your business might start out with just you working it, but as you grow, the importance of those other people will become more and more crucial.

Surround yourself with excellence to drive you to even greater heights of accomplishment, and never forget to thank the people who have helped you create your business. With every company I invest in, I insist that they tie their key employees into the equity so they share a piece of the pie. To me, that is a sign of the health of a company and the integrity of its leaders. You have to make sure that you show due respect and appreciation to the people who have contributed to your success, or you'll risk becoming the boss who hears, "I don't have time for this job anymore . . ."

 **Are you ready to achieve that dream you've always had? Then this is the time to act. This is the moment to take that first step to make it happen. This is the moment to finally change your life.**

But as we discussed at the outset, entrepreneurship isn't for everyone. There are some people who just aren't risk takers or who struggle to see beyond the present to the possibilities of the future. And then, of course, there are some people who simply don't understand how entrepreneurs think. It's not just about mastering your environment or making money. No matter what your driver is, no matter what your motivation or passion, I have yet to meet a successful entrepreneur who wasn't most excited about the prospect of achieving something great, and in many cases, something greater than him- or herself.

Whether it's an industry-changing advancement, like the computer code that Paul Allen and Bill Gates concocted in a small hotel room in Albuquerque back in 1977 and that grew to become Microsoft, or a local restaurant that becomes a gathering place for good food and good memories for families in the community, the point is that entrepreneurs are people who want to do more than the ordinary day-in-day-out drudgery of life. They share a common goal of creating something bigger than themselves, and they share the fact that they all took that first leap of faith to actually make it happen.

Where are you today? Are you ready to step out into the unknown armed with just a plan and a will to succeed? Are you ready for some short-term sacrifices on behalf of long-term gains? Are you ready to make the most of an economy that has left countless motivated and skilled workers champing at the bit for a job with a boss and a company that will treat them right? Are you ready to achieve that dream you've always had? Then this is the time to act. This is the moment to take that first step to make it happen. This is the moment to finally change your life.

A few years ago, I was driving down the street in Montreal, Canada, having just come from breakfast at a little French café. I was relishing the incredible travel and networking experiences that my work has brought when I stopped to check my BlackBerry while waiting at a red light.

There were a few e-mails from people I knew who had seen my recent appearance on the Donny Deutsch show and were writing to congratulate me, which of course made me feel great—and then I opened a letter that threw me for a loop. It was very short, saying simply, "I am proud of you. You should know that your grandmother is very ill."

Staring at that tiny screen, I was mystified. It didn't seem to be from any of my siblings or my mom. Was it some distant relative? Who would be writing me something like that? And then I scrolled down and my eyes fell on the most unbelievable word in the signature: "Dad." My dad had sent me an e-mail. The man who had been gone from my life without a trace for nearly fifteen years—no Christmas cards or calls on my birthday or child support checks to my mom—just a complete void from the day he disappeared. And now he was writing to me.

I pulled my car over immediately as a torrent of emotions swept over me. I mean, I had waited literally over half of my life for this moment to reconnect with him, and now that opportunity was sitting in the palm of my hand. The intervening years had allowed me to pass through all the stages of hurt and anger that I felt toward him—not just for what he had done to my mom and to me, but for what he had done to ruin himself and the life he had built. But as time passed, I had finally been able to let go of all of that, and I wanted tell him that I forgave him and loved him, but I'd never known how to reach him. Until now.

This is yet another reason that I am fascinated by modern technology; less than one minute after his original message came in to me, I was typing out a response to him that was almost fifteen years in the making. I told him that I owed my success to the character traits he'd taught me as a child: work ethic and ambition. I told him I wanted him to sleep peacefully at night knowing that I was thankful for those lessons he had given me. And I told him he would always be my father, and I'd always be his son.

Because of that day, I began to write the first half of my life story, called *Faith of the Dots, A Story of Nothing to Lose*. The title was inspired from a speech that Steve Jobs, the founder of Apple, gave at Stanford University about how our lives are a series of unrelated events until we connect them. The subtitle is my mantra in life and the title of this book. During my growing up years, authorities used to say, "Ryan Blair acts like he has nothing to lose, so you better watch out for him." They were right, because people with nothing to lose will take unreasonable action; they're not afraid of the consequences or of failure. They will stop at nothing. This mindset channeled positively is how I enter every new venture I jump into. And I suggest you do the same.

With *Faith of the Dots*, I started with a list of 200 of my most vivid memories, as a mnemonic device. As the chapters assembled themselves, I realized that the return of my father was the event that would enable me to become a father myself and embrace fatherhood with a sense of responsibility. I wouldn't repeat the vicious cycle of abuse. I wanted to forgive the man who was so evil to me and my family and remove the emotional scar tissue, as well as the behavioral patterns he burned into me. Most important, I wanted my son, Ryan Reagan Blair, to begin his dots unbound by his father's—and his grandfather's—limitations. I wanted him to start his life free of the ghosts that haunt this family's past and to be proud of his name.

The moment my father contacted me was one that changed both of our lives forever. He began to reconcile with his past, and I was finally able to start a new chapter of peace. We were in constant e-mail communication from that point forward, and we still are, but we still haven't talked or met in person. Perhaps as I complete the book *Faith of the Dots*, I'll pick up the phone and arrange to sit down with him. Maybe I will be able to tell him "Happy Father's Day" for the first time since I was a kid, something that has really stayed with me for some reason.

I learned something else from my father that day in Montreal when he reentered my life, something tied to those same childhood lessons on industriousness and tenacity that he'd instilled in me so long ago—I learned the importance of forcing myself to go forward with something that seems frightening or intimidating or a huge risk. It turns out that my dad had been wanting to contact me for a long time but wasn't sure how I'd react. He finally decided to just do it because he realized he'd never know what would happen if he didn't try.

That resolve really impressed me because it reminded me of how important it truly is to take that first step. It's true with our relationships, and it's true in business. You have to be willing to go forward with a plan, as scary as that can be, because it's the only way to have a chance at reaching your goal. As the saying goes, "You miss 100 percent of the shots you never take."

Life is full of unknowns. If we allowed fear to hold us back from every decision whose outcome was unsure, we'd be paralyzed into a life of absolute inaction. We'd never accomplish anything. Things may not always work out the way we planned—they might even come to nothing, but they might exceed anything we ever imagined.

My dad understood that, and he took the risk to reconnect with me. His first e-mail that day reminded me of the most important thing a person can remember as he or she seeks to enter the world of entrepreneurship. By making the decision to act, to make a change, to go forward, to take that risk, you have nothing to lose—and everything in the world to gain.

NOTES: _____

NOTES: _____

NOTHING to LOSE
Start-Up Weekend!
August 27th–30th

Got an IDEA? Get STARTED.

Announcing a competition for all entrepreneurs, where chosen applicants will be invited to Los Angeles to pitch their business idea to Ryan Blair and the Nothing to Lose team of advisors. The finalists will get three days of mentorship from an elite team of venture capitalists, PR experts, and internet marketing professionals, who will give their honest analysis of each business plan. At the end of the competition, we plan to fund a minimum of three start-ups.

There is no limit on the amount of funding we're providing—some companies need 10K to get started and some need 500K; others may need help creating a profitable business plan and given access to a larger group of investors. This is not a competition where everyone wins or is guaranteed a certain amount of financing. This is real business.

The competition is open to verified U.S. residents, and all business plans will be considered. Applicants should register online at nothingtolose.com, study the book *Nothing to Lose*, and show how they have mastered and applied the principles, lessons, and philosophies of the material in their business plans. E-mail us at: startupweekend@nothingtolose.com with 'Start-Up' in the title to receive an application, or register and apply online at nothingtolose.com.

NOTHING to LOSE

Want to get the latest updates and news from Nothing to Lose Publishing? Learn more at:

www.NothingtoLose.com

And don't miss out on the chance to network with like-minded entrepreneurs in the Nothing to Lose community on Twitter and Facebook.

www.twitter.com/ntlpublishing   **www.facebook.com/ntlpublishing**

Support the Book!

Please support the book and help the people in your network create more American jobs. We're tracking the results of our social media campaign (Facebook, Twitter, Amazon reviews) and our biggest supporters will be seriously considered for the Nothing to Lose Start-Up Weekend funding competition.

If you liked the book, please start by tweeting the following:

Love @Ryan_Blair's book *Nothing to Lose*.
Check it out at http://ntlpublishing.com.